OUTSTANDING STAGE MONOLOGS AND SCENES FROM THE '90s

Professional Auditions for Student Actors

EDITED BY
STEVEN H. GALE

MERIWETHER PUBLISHING LTD.
Colorado Springs, Colorado

Meriwether Publishing Ltd., Publisher
P.O. Box 7710
Colorado Springs, CO 80933

Executive editor: Theodore O. Zapel
Typesetting: Elisabeth Hendricks
Cover design: Janice Melvin

Library of Congress Cataloging-in-Publication Data

Outstanding stage monologs and scenes from the 90's / edited by Steven H. Gale
    p. cm.
   ISBN 1-56608-058-4 (pbk.)
    1. Monologues. 2. Drama--20th century. 3. Acting--Auditions. I. Gale, Steven H.

PN2080 .O88 2000
822'.04508'0904--dc21

00-028062
CIP

1 2 3 4 5   00 01 02 03

Contents

Thematic Table of Contents

Acknowledgments

In 1998 I approached Ted Zapel, editor at Meriwether Publishing, with a proposal for a book. Although he decided that the volume did not fit the current needs of the Meriwether program, he suggested that I might consider compiling a collection of scenes and monologs for actors. I liked his suggestions, and over a period of some months, we discussed and refined the concept. *Outstanding Stage Monologs and Scenes from the '90s* was the result of those discussions. For his original suggestion and for his help in developing the concepts that lie behind this book, I am extremely grateful.

There was a considerable amount of labor that went into *Outstanding Stage Monologs and Scenes from the '90s*, and a lot of that work was made easier for me by my secretary, Kim Bickers. Kim helped me locate plays, she photocopied the selections that I made, and she sent out the permissions requests and recorded the responses. When we did not hear from someone, or she had to track them down because they were no longer at a given address, or when we had to negotiate terms — all of the indispensable minutiae that go into such a project over an extended period of time — she made sure that everything was taken care of, spending countless hours on the telephone or Internet and faxing back and forth. I truly appreciate this invaluable help.

Lori Muha at the Paul Blazer Library at Kentucky State University was especially diligent in helping me locate copies of plays, for which I am thankful.

I would also like to acknowledge the love and support of my family, colleagues, and friends.

As always, I want to thank my wife, Kathy, and my three daughters, Shannon, Ashley, and Heather, for their motivation, inspiration, and help, and especially for their patience.

Introduction

Actors need to be able to use proven examples of good dramatic material to practice their craft. That is clearly the primary concept underlying the creation of any scene book. The selections that I made in designing *Outstanding Stage Monologs and Scenes from the '90s* obviously mirror this fact (witness the names of some of those included: Harold Pinter, Edward Albee, Thornton Wilder, Tom Stoppard, Mario Fratti, A. J. Gurney, Brian Friel, Marsha Norman, Israel Horovitz). Besides these established and famous playwrights, the list of authors includes young, up-and-coming dramatists as well, writers whose early works will produce the foundation for significant careers.

As might be expected, I have included scenes and monologs for one male actor, one female actor, two male actors, two female actors, and combinations of male and female actors. In addition, though, the forty-three pieces by thirty-nine dramatists that I chose for this volume reflect actors' desires for new and fresh scenes and monologs, pieces that are up-to-date and exciting to perform — thus, the '90s. And the decade of the '90s serves as an important and rich launching point. During this period, several trends became evident. Small theatre groups are proliferating, more women are writing plays, ethnic and racial groups are exerting a growing influence on what is produced on stage, young authors are turning to drama as a medium for expression, and drama is truly an international art form. These trends are represented in this volume.

In choosing to include only scenes, monologs, and short dramas written in or first produced in the 1990s, I could capture the closing out of the millennium. I could encompass many of the changes taking place in the theatre that serve as a summary of the twentieth century. These changes involve the elements mentioned above, of course, but they also mean a wider variety of backgrounds represented than ever before, and the impact of a sub-genre that is coming into its own with the emergence of the ten-minute play. Ten-minute plays are now afforded their rightful place beside full-length and one-act plays in the theatre since national festivals have been devoted to this format in Kentucky, Delaware, and several other states. This allows new and expanded opportunities for

1

actors to utilize meaningful, interesting, and pertinent matter in auditions, readings, practices, performances, and the like. This particular element is what lies behind my decision to incorporate five complete ten-minute plays in this volume. Given the international nature of the theatre and recognizing that influences are no longer limited by national borders, I have also included a few selections from abroad — from Cameroon, Canada, England, Ireland, France, and Germany.

Finally, as a quick glance at the table of contents will show, this volume was structured to make it easy to find pieces for class use or auditions; the sections are divided according to gender, and within each section the order of the selections is from shortest to longest.

I hope that the practitioners of the thespian arts who use the selections contained in *Outstanding Stage Monologs and Scenes from the '90s* enjoy using them as much as I enjoyed collecting them.

Steven H. Gale
Frankfort, Kentucky
January 2000

NOTE: The numerals running vertically down the left margin of each page of dialog are for the convenience of the director. With these, he/she may easily direct attention to a specific passage.

Scenes for
One Female

Ashes to Ashes
by Harold Pinter

1   British dramatist Harold Pinter is considered by many to be the
2 most important English-language playwright of the twentieth
3 century, and he is internationally acclaimed both for his individual
4 plays and for his indelible influence on world theatre. Many of his
5 dramas, including *The Caretaker*, *The Homecoming*, *Landscape*,
6 and *Old Times*, have already been accorded the status of classics of
7 the modern theatre. In *Ashes to Ashes*, which premiered at the
8 Royal Court Theatre in London in 1996, a woman is haunted by
9 the memories of her experiences during a holocaust.

10

11

12 **REBECCA: Oh, by the way, there's something I meant to**
13   **tell you. I was standing in a room at the top of a very**
14   **tall building in the middle of town. The sky was full of**
15   **stars. I was about to close the curtains but I stayed at**
16   **the window for a time looking up at the stars. Then I**
17   **looked down. I saw an old man and a little boy**
18   **walking down the street. They were both dragging**
19   **suitcases. The little boy's suitcase was bigger than he**
20   **was. It was a very bright night. Because of the stars.**
21   **The old man and the little boy were walking down the**
22   **street. They were holding each other's free hand. I**
23   **wondered where they were going. Anyway, I was**
24   **about to close the curtains but then I suddenly saw a**
25   **woman following them, carrying a baby in her arms.**
26   *(Pause)* **Did I tell you the street was icy? It was icy. So**
27   **she had to tread very carefully. Over the bumps. The**
28   **stars were out. She followed the man and the boy**
29   **until they turned the corner and were gone.** *(Pause)*
30   **She stood still. She kissed her baby. The baby was a**

1   girl. *(Pause)* **She kissed her.** *(Pause)* **She listened to**
2   **the baby's heartbeat. The baby's heart was beating.**
3   *(The light in the room has darkened. The lamps are very*
4   *bright. REBECCA sits very still.)* **The baby was**
5   **breathing.** *(Pause)* **I held her to me. She was**
6   **breathing. Her heart was beating. They took us to**
7   **the trains**
8 ECHO: the trains
9 REBECCA: They were taking the babies away
10 ECHO: the babies away *(Pause)*
11 REBECCA: I took my baby and wrapped it in my shawl
12 ECHO: my shawl
13 REBECCA: And I made it into a bundle
14 ECHO: a bundle
15 REBECCA: And I held it under my left arm
16 ECHO: my left arm *(Pause)*
17 REBECCA: And I went through with my baby
18 ECHO: my baby *(Pause)*
19 REBECCA: But the baby cried out
20 ECHO: cried out
21 REBECCA: And the man called me back
22 ECHO: called me back
23 REBECCA: And he said what do you have there
24 ECHO: have there
25 REBECCA: He stretched out his hand for the bundle
26 ECHO: for the bundle
27 REBECCA: And I gave him the bundle
28 ECHO: the bundle
29 REBECCA: And that's the last time I held the bundle
30 ECHO: the bundle *(Silence)*
31 REBECCA: And we got on the train
32 ECHO: the train
33 REBECCA: And we arrived at this place
34 ECHO: this place
35 REBECCA: And I met a woman I knew

1   ECHO: I knew
2   REBECCA: And she said what happened to your baby
3   ECHO: your baby
4   REBECCA: Where is your baby
5   ECHO: your baby
6   REBECCA: And I said what baby
7   ECHO: what baby
8   REBECCA: I don't have a baby
9   ECHO: a baby
10 REBECCA: I don't know of any baby
11 ECHO: of any baby *(Pause)*
12 REBECCA: I don't know of any baby *(Long silence)*
13 BLACKOUT
14
15
16
17
18
19
20
21
22
23
24
25
26
27
28
29
30
31
32
33
34
35 **Echo might be deleted for a dramatic reading.

A Cheever Evening

by A. R. Gurney

1   A.R. Gurney is one of America's most popular contemporary
2 dramatists; his award-winning *Love Letters* is a perennial favorite
3 among touring companies. In *A Cheever Evening*, a woman recites
4 the events of a typical day in her empty life.
5
6
7   **CHRISTINA:** *(To audience)* **Lately my husband and I have**
8   **had trouble getting to sleep. Burt is temporarily**
9   **unemployed, so he relaxes by taking long walks**
10   **around the neighborhood. As for me? Why I simply**
11   **review what I've done during the course of the day.**
12   **This morning, for example, I drove Burt to the early**
13   **train so he could look for another job. Then I ...**
14   *(Consults her notebook.)* **Had the skis repaired. Booked**
15   **a tennis court. Bought the wine and groceries because**
16   **tonight was our turn to give the monthly dinner of the**
17   **Société Gastronomique du Westchester Nord.**
18   **Attended a League of Women Voters meeting on**
19   **sewers. Went to a full-dress lunch for Bobsie Neil's**
20   **aunt. Weeded the garden. Ironed a uniform for the**
21   **part-time maid who helped with the dinner. Typed two**
22   **and a half pages of my paper for the Book Club on the**
23   **early novels of Henry James. Emptied the**
24   **wastebaskets. Helped the sitter prepare the children's**
25   **supper. Gave Ronny some batting practice. Put**
26   **Lizzie's hair in pin curls. Got the cook. Met Burt at**
27   **five-thirty-five. Took a bath. Dressed. Greeted our**
28   **guests in French at half past seven. Said *bon soir* to**
29   **all at eleven and that's about it.** *(Puts her notebook*
30   *away.)* **Some people might say I am prideful for**

1   **accomplishing all this. I don't think so. All I really**
2   **am is a woman enjoying herself in a country that is**
3   **prosperous and still young.** *(Burt comes on, again in*
4   *dark clothes.)* **Coming to bed darling?**
5
6
7
8
9
10
11
12
13
14
15
16
17
18
19
20
21
22
23
24
25
26
27
28
29
30
31
32
33
34
35

Blink of an Eye
by Jeremy Dobrish

1   A guardian angel discusses her job with people and cats in
2 Jeremy Dobrish's *Blink of an Eye*.
3
4
5 **CELESTE: Well, you see, being a Guardian Angel is not the**
6   **greatest job you could ever ask for. I mean, yes, you**
7   **get certain perks. Stopping time's not bad, free fries,**
8   **whatever, but basically it's a pretty low self-esteem**
9   **kind of a deal. No matter how hard you try, you're**
10   **destined to fail right? I mean I can watch and watch**
11   **and watch, and be your guardian and help out as best**
12   **I can. But ultimately, one of these days (and I'm not**
13   **saying it's coming anytime soon OK? so don't get all**
14   **freaky and weird on me) but one of these days**
15   **someone or something's gonna act too quickly for me**
16   **to react and you're gonna get yours.**
17
18   . . .
19   **I mean it's not like you're my only client you know**
20   **what I'm saying? I've got a lot of people to look out**
21   **for. Not to mention the animals, although I must**
22   **admit the cats are a little easier cause at least I can**
23   **blow it a few times with them so I don't really watch**
24   **my cats too closely ... Oh, but don't get me wrong ...,**
25   **I like cats. People ..., they try to be in the past,**
26   **present and future all at the same time, while cats live**
27   **only in the present, in the eternity of an instant. Ever**
28   **notice that?**
29
30

The Heart of a Child
by Eric Lane

1   *The Heart of a Child* by Eric Lane premiered in New York City
2   at the Orange Thoughts Theater and Film in 1991. Carrying their
3   newborn baby, a woman visits the grave of her husband, a pilot
4   killed in the South Pacific in World War II, as well as the grave of
5   her father-in-law.
6
7
8   MARY ALICE: I named him Isaac. Everybody thinking I'm
9   gonna name him Jimmy John, but I called him Isaac
10   so that his time come, the Lord'll reach down and
11   spare my son. *(To John, her father-in-law)* I remember
12   how you be talking how when one soul dies, a child's
13   born for him to enter. Well, that's nonsense. A soul
14   goes to heaven or hell. But not in my child. *(To Jimmy,*
15   *her husband)* They give me your dog tags. And your
16   medals. Some you didn't even tell me. Radio
17   mechanic. *(Smiles.)* I would've liked to've seen that.
18   And for your missions. They give me them and I keep
19   them, but they don't mean nothing to me without you.
20   I know I ain't supposed to say that but it's true. I miss
21   you so much. I know you been away and maybe I
22   thought I'd be used to it, but that was different 'cause
23   I always knew you were coming back. I love you so
24   much. I love you both. You like his name, don't you?
25   *(Sings name.)* I-saac. I-saac. He's got your eyes. And his
26   own soul. *(Whispers.)* Isaac.
27
28
29
30

The Queen's Knight
by Frank Cossa

1   It is October 1793 in Paris and Marie-Antoinette, the former
2 Queen of France faces death in Frank Cossa's *The Queen's*
3 *Knight.*
4
5
6 QUEEN: I have been a prisoner of these people for four
7   years. I watched them march to the gates of the
8   palace and slaughter six hundred Swiss guards. I
9   watched as all my friends were murdered or driven
10   into exile. I watched them execute my husband who
11   was their King. I watched them drag my children
12   screaming from my arms so that after a year I don't
13   know if they're alive or dead. I have lived in this room
14   for seventy-six days. They allow me two dresses, no
15   undergarments, no cloak, no blanket against the
16   dampness that runs down the walls. There is never
17   any fire wood. There is always a guard outside my cell
18   who must keep his eyes on me at all times. At all
19   times. Some days ago the Princess de Lamballe, my
20   last loyal friend, returned from a safe exile to be near
21   me in my difficult time. She came here to visit me. The
22   mob saw her and I watched them tear her to pieces.
23   Her head was impaled on a stake and raised up to my
24   window there. *(She points.)* One man made himself
25   moustaches out of her private hair while the others,
26   laughing and cheering, threw parts of her ... her body
27   up at me. You see, monsieur, for four years one
28   horror has followed another. They have allowed me
29   no comfort, no rest. They have spared me no cruelty,
30   no shock, no terror. And you wish me to ask these

1   **people for ...** *(She turns, slowly again, to look at him.)*
2   **a favor?**
3
4
5
6
7
8
9
10
11
12
13
14
15
16
17
18
19
20
21
22
23
24
25
26
27
28
29
30
31
32
33
34
35

The Most Massive Woman Wins

by Madeleine George

1   A seventeen-year-old girl in a liposuction clinic waiting room
2   ruminates in *The Most Massive Woman Wins* by Madeleine
3   George.
4
5
6   **RENNIE: The first picture of me is at my first birthday**
7   **party. In this one I am screaming with laughter and**
8   **holding my hands up to show the camera that I am**
9   **covered with chocolate cake. My face is smeared with**
10 **it, it is all over the front of my pretty pink dress.**
11 **Apparently I was quite verbally advanced, and my**
12 **parents were showing me off when my Uncle Jake**
13 **said, "Oh yeah? How smart is she?" "She's a genius,"**
14 **says my mother, "she understands everything. Try it.**
15 **She'll do anything you say." So ... "Rennie," says my**
16 **Uncle Jake, "smush that chocolate cake all over your**
17 **face, sweetheart. Will you do that for me?" And I did**
18 **it, of course, because I was just that smart and I**
19 **ruined my dress and they took a picture of me**
20 **humiliating myself when I was twelve months old.**
21 *(Flashbulb pops.)* **This one is my mother's favorite. It's**
22 **of her and me on one of our mother-daughter days,**
23 **we're on the steps of the Met looking very close and**
24 **what you don't see is Mother boring her knuckles into**
25 **the small of my back saying "Straighten up,**
26 **sweetheart, it lengthens your neck. Now glow, come**
27 **on, glow. We want this one to glow." For awhile there**
28 **is an absence of photos — when tummies are no**
29 **longer little-girl cute. Mother hides me at family**
30 **gatherings and I seem always to end up behind pieces**

1   of furniture. So we have no extant record of the
2   long years of wanting, of wanting and wanting and
3   being denied. Reaching for bread and peanut butter
4   and having Slimfast thrust into my twelve-year-old
5   fist. Mother says "No, I am putting my foot down."
6   She is putting her foot down, I see, and I see that
7   to want and demand things is bad.
8
9
10
11
12
13
14
15
16
17
18
19
20
21
22
23
24
25
26
27
28
29
30
31
32
33
34
35

Alicia Maria Gets a Job at the Bakery
by Joan Lipkin

1   An immigrant is plagued by the challenges of the English
2 language and a night job in Joan Lipkin's *Alicia Maria Gets a Job*
3 *at the Bakery.*
4
5
6 **ALICIA MARIA: I didn't always work at the bank. I used to**
7   **work at the bakery. I had went to this bakery to buy**
8   **bread. At this time, my English is not so good and I**
9   **didn't know that supermarkets are for bread, bakeries**
10   **are for birthday cakes. But no matter what language**
11   **you speak, a big white cardboard sign in the window**
12   **means maybe they are hiring. So I ask for a job. They**
13   **say, do you have any experience in bakeries? I say,**
14   **yes, I bake bread all the time. They say, no, do you**
15   **have any experience *working* in a bakery? I say, no.**
16   **They say, how about selling? I say, oh, yes! That is**
17   **how I come to this country. On the boat. Selling. They**
18   **say, no. Not *sailing*. *Selling*. To customers. By now,**
19   **these two ladies, Astrid and Ingrid, are starting to**
20   **cluck their tongues. They are clucking so loud, I**
21   **almost look to see where the chickens are. And I am**
22   **so hungry, I could eat the plastic models in the display**
23   **case. I say, I know my English is not so good but I am**
24   **going to night school to learn better. Maybe there are**
25   **people who come in here whose English is also not so**
26   **good so we speak the same language. They are not so**
27   **sure. So I say, then put me in the back. I sweep the**
28   **floors. You show me? I do it. Because I love bread. I**
29   **eat so many sandwiches, I have a special feeling for**
30   **this work. So Astrid says to Ingrid, or maybe it is**

Ingrid who says to Astrid, you know we are having a hard time getting someone for the graveyard shift. We could maybe try her out. And they hire me! Now I know why they are calling it the graveyard shift. Because it is killing me. I am also going to night school so I can speak better the English. By the time I get to the bakery, I am very tired and my head is full of the verbs. But, *Dios mio*, I am happy. It is not much money, eh? But it is *something*, plus all the burnt bread and broken cookies I can eat! Instead of going hungry, my only worry is now the weight. *Gracias el cielo!* America is really something.

Fragments

by John Jay Garrett

1 John Jay Garrett's *Fragments* is about events during the life
2 and death of Jack Wilson. In this selection, Wilson's mother recalls
3 learning about his death in Vietnam.
4
5
6 MAUREEN: I told myself I wasn't going to talk at this
7   meeting, but I guess I always say that. I just wanted
8   to respond to Janet's question. No Janet, not at all. I
9   remember I used to sit at the kitchen table and stare
10   at the door for what seemed like hours, waiting for
11   the doorbell to ring. Sometimes, I'd even stand at the
12   front window, expecting a government car to pull up.
13   And it seemed that every time the doorbell would ring,
14   I had forgotten to expect it. My heart would go all
15   fluttery on me and I'd hate myself for not being
16   prepared. I used to pore over his letters for days,
17   looking for every clue into his life there, what sort of
18   changes it was forcing upon him. I remember he
19   would sometimes tell me about KIAs and WIAs and I
20   almost fooled myself into thinking it was like his high
21   school soccer scores. *(Smiles.)* I guess you know what
22   I mean. And all that was before my husband found me
23   in line at the DMV and told me Jack was dead. One of
24   the first things I started to do after I found out was go
25   to the airport. I started going three times a week,
26   sometimes four. I used to stand there with a small
27   flag, not because I believed in the war, or the
28   government, but just so the boys coming home knew
29   someone back here cared about them coming home
30   alive, mourned for what they had gone through. I was

1   arrested once when I punched a girl who had just
2   spat on one of them. Knocked her right in the nose.
3   I felt like a real jerk afterward. Here I am, a forty-
4   three-year-old woman, hitting some kid who
5   doesn't really know what she's doing. But it just
6   made me so mad when I saw the look on that poor
7   boy's face. I kept going to the airport until seventy-
8   three. Sometimes I'd tell them that I loved them, or
9   give them a hug, but mostly I just . . . mostly I just
10   imagined that I was waiting for Jack. *(Pause.)* **No,**
11   **Janet. I don't believe you think about him too**
12   **much. I believe everyone else thinks about them**
13   **too little.**
14
15
16
17
18
19
20
21
22
23
24
25
26
27
28
29
30
31
32
33
34
35

Down by the Ocean
by P. J. Barry

1   P. J. Barry's *Down by the Ocean* is about a woman whose
2 husband has suffered a stroke. In this scene she brings him up-to-
3 date about the family.

4

5

6 **LIL:** *(Setting him in place)* **Isn't it a perfect day? Just perfect!**
7   *(Pause)* **I'm so glad I got my swim in. You know me. I**
8   **have to get my swim in or I'm not happy.** *(Sits at a TV*
9   *table with string beans, a pot, etc.)* **I'll bet they're all in**
10   **again ... at least Ann and Betsy. Not Alice, of course.**
11   **You know what she's doing, the scamp.** *(Laughs, strings*
12   *beans.)* **You comfortable, honeybun?** *(Pause)* **Good.**
13   *(Pause)* **You are my honeybun ... always ... always ...**
14   *(Sings.)* **Always.** *(Smiles.)* **On our honeymoon ... that's**
15   **when you first called me honeybun ... I stole it from**
16   **you.** *(Pause)* **I was so frightened. I kept talking ...**
17   **chatter, chatter, chatter ... and you said: "Stop**
18   **talking, honeybun ... just kiss me" ... and I heard you**
19   **take off your glasses and then you kissed me.** *(Giggles.)*
20   **Oh, you were so sweet ... so loving ... oh, my!** *(Giggles*
21   *again.)* **You like it out here, don't you? Like David —**
22   **God rest his soul. He loved this porch, too ... loved**
23   **the view ... the way you do.** *(Sighs.)* **David and Connie**
24   **both gone now — God rest their souls. So sad ...** *(Sings*
25   *loudly.)* **"Sad, sad and lonely ... sad. Sad and blue ..."**
26   *(Now Peter is revived by Lil's singing.)* **And so we bought**
27   **their summer place for us and our children ... but Lilly**
28   **and hers ... so far away. Why anybody would want to**
29   **live in Michigan is beyond me. Oh, Peter. I seldom**
30   **refer to them as Little Lil and Little Peter anymore.**

1   Aren't you proud of me? *(Pause)* I know you are. At
2   least Lilly gave us grandchildren. I don't think Peter
3   ever will. He's only dated a handful of girls in the
4   last seven or eight years. Let's see. There were
5   four. Anita ... Helen ... Roberta ... wait, I skipped
6   one. It was an M. *(Beat)* M ... *(Beat)* Maxine! Oh,
7   Maxine was a thousand years ago ... she spoke
8   several languages ... What a memory! Still. There is
9   hope, honeybun. *(Peter begins to nod off to sleep again*
10   *and soon succeeds.)* Last week when he wrote and
11   said he was a volunteer for Kennedy ... well, I was
12   overjoyed! Of course, he's attached himself to a
13   losing battle, a Catholic can't win the presidency.
14   But from now until November our son will most
15   likely meet some pretty girl, most likely Catholic ...
16   so many of those volunteers for Kennedy will be.
17   *(Pause)* Keep your fingers crossed. *(Stops stringing*
18   *the beans. Sighs.)* You change their diapers and
19   bathe them and powder them and kiss them and
20   feed them ... and change their diapers and bathe
21   them and powder them ... and sing to them ...
22   *(Slightly teary-eyed, sings three lines of a lullaby. Pause.)*
23   ... and then they talk ... and walk ... and they're in
24   school ... in college ... and married ... or whatever
25   ... and gone. *(Sings with more volume, awakening*
26   *Peter.)* "Gone are the days ... When our hearts were
27   young and gay ..." *(Pause. Thoughtfully)* And here we
28   are, sugarplum, together in our summer place
29   which was to be for them and their children ...
30   *(Pause)* They come back home so seldom ... Little Lil
31   ... Little Peter ... *(Resumes stringing beans. With*
32   *practicality)* We are selling. It's on the market, I told
33   you. Isabelle, next door, made us an offer. She said
34   she'd stop by this afternoon ... to chat. *(Peter*
35   *appears more interested.)* I've never liked that girl.

1 **She still flaunts herself. Oh, she does.** *(Pause)* **She**
2 **appears to be a good mother, but I'm afraid she's**
3 **...** *(Whispers)* **... basically a tramp.** *(Turning to him)*
4 **You know I wouldn't use that word unless I felt it**
5 **was hitting the nail right on the head.** *(Peter is*
6 *managing a slight gesture.)* **What is it? Is that sweater**
7 **a little heavy now?** *(Rises, goes to him.)* **I think so.**
8 **Well, we'll be rid of that problem in a jiffy, my**
9 **handsome husband.** *(Begins to get him out of it.)*
10 **Handsome, honeybun. Sugarplum. You are.** *(Kisses*
11 *his cheek.)* **I see the glint in your eye.**
12
13
14
15
16
17
18
19
20
21
22
23
24
25
26
27
28
29
30
31
32
33
34
35

Glass Stirring

by Eric Lane

1 *Glass Stirring* by Eric Lane was originally produced at the
2 Orange Thoughts Theater and Film in New York City in 1990. The
3 drama is about an American family that loses a son in World War II.
4
5
6 JEAN: The Lord is my Shepherd; I shall not want. I miss
7   Johnny. Church had a Bake Sale Sunday to raise
8   money for a memorial they want to build, for all the
9   boys. Everybody's been saving what they can but with
10   the rations, cakes don't taste the same—except Mrs.
11   Harris. Her sister sends her her canning points from
12   the City, so her pies are sweet as before the War. One
13   thing about a Bake Sale now, it all goes. Mrs.
14   Thompson, she made that apple pan dowdy she does.
15   Her boy Jimmy was there wearing Johnny's coat. I
16   gave it to him. I didn't think I was favoring him, I just
17   knew they were the same size. Looked real good in it,
18   too. I asked the Preacher, he said they'd give away the
19   rest to boys in need. I still don't know what we're
20   gonna do with Johnny's room. I go in there and it's
21   like I feel him, in the walls, the headboard of that bed.
22   Preacher's talking Armageddon. I must've heard that
23   passage a hundred times, then one day it just makes
24   sense. War's going on longer than anybody expected.
25   Sunday night we had another air-raid drill. Whole
26   house sealed tight, that blue army blanket over the
27   window so no lights coming out. So the Japanese
28   won't be able to tell us from the woods. Agnes, she's
29   trying to get us to come down to the dance hall.
30   Daddy, he won't go. "Momma," he tells me. "You

27

1   want to go you go alone." We went that one time —
2   he just sat there looking out. Agnes and me, we
3   danced. She's real good, too. Knows how to lead
4   and everything. All those songs they're playing
5   about you leaving me and dreaming the rest. Daddy
6   thought it was loud, but not if you're dancing. I
7   know Johnny liked to dance. I still don't know what
8   we're gonna do with that room. Preacher's giving
9   out the clothes and the books, but I still feel him. I
10   even knew when he died the moment it happened.
11   Preacher's up there reading about Lot and his wife
12   leaving the burning city. And just when he gets to
13   the part where she turns to look back — everything
14   stops. I see Jesus behind him on the cross looking
15   down and it's like he's looking right at me and then
16   he lights up — Jesus. None of the apostles or Mary
17   — just Jesus. The light through the glass — pieces
18   of red, blue, the brown in his beard, all lit. And
19   looking down at me. I hear an airplane over and I
20   know the Lord's taken my boy. Nobody else sees.
21   And I don't say nothing. I know if I do they'll tell me
22   it was just a cloud passing by or a shadow from the
23   plane but I know it was Johnny — Next day the
24   telegram came. We buried him out in the family
25   plot. Agnes, she planted tulips. Goes every Sunday
26   after church with me and Daddy to see if they come
27   up yet. Sometimes I feel like that house during air
28   raid, all boarded up and no light showing through.
29   The Lord giveth; and the Lord taketh away. I know
30   he told Lot's wife not to look back, but maybe she
31   just couldn't see nothing ahead.
32
33
34
35

The Ride

by Bridget Carpenter

1   In this selection from *The Ride*, Bridget Carpenter's elderly
2 character reminisces about car rides with her husband and her dog,
3 Sparky.
4
5
6 **ALICE: I put some old hamburger in there tonight.** *(She*
7   *hands an imaginary bowl to Sparky, who takes it between*
8   *his teeth and places it on the floor. He sniffs suspiciously.*
9   *ALICE speaks partially to herself.)* **Hamburger was**
10   **Frank's favorite meal. He never liked anything fancy.**
11   **He could eat a hamburger every night. "Alice, you**
12   **should start a chain like McDonalds," he would**
13   **always say. He picked you out, you know. You were**
14   **the scrawniest looking pup of Maddie McPherson's**
15   **dog's litter. Frank just saw you and said, "I bet this**
16   **one likes hamburger too, think so, Alice?" I said I**
17   **thought so. And we took you home. By then Betsy had**
18   **already grown up, and I wasn't in the wheelchair yet.**
19   **Remember? That was when we went on some great**
20   **rides.** *(ALICE holds out her hand. Sparky does not see*
21   *this, but he knows it is there, and he leaves his food to go*
22   *to ALICE and be petted. She pats him vigorously.)* **When**
23   **Frank didn't mind driving all day to get to a really**
24   **good roller coaster. You loved those car rides. And**
25   **those coasters! Such wonderful long rides ... every**
26   **coaster with an exciting name ... the Phoenix.**
27   **Hercules. Screaming Eagle. Le Mistral. Dragon Fyre.**
28   **And Frank could never convince the operator to let**
29   **you get on the coaster with us — even though he tried**
30   **every time. "Let the dog have some fun!" he would**

1 shout. But you never got to ride. Just watched from
2 the ground, barking to beat the band. You'd make
3 such a fuss! And Frank would always yell at the ride
4 operator after it was over. "You should have let the
5 dog come!" he'd say. Oh, my. And you were even
6 worse after we joined the American Roller Coaster
7 Enthusiasts' Club. All those parks where we were
8 allowed Unlimited Ride Time ... and we'd ride until
9 we were dizzy ... and the wind rushed past our ears
10 as we flew through the air ... the wind! Lifting us
11 up, carrying us beyond earthly sadness or pain.
12 Whshhh! Whshhh ... whshhh ... whshhh ... *(She*
13 *raises her arms slightly, as if on a coaster.)* ... And you'd
14 just sit and bark. You were such a worried puppy,
15 watching us go! The trip home, Frank would always
16 sing, "When Irish Eyes Are Smiling ..." So sweet.
17 So sweetly. And he'd always say, "If only the dog
18 could've taken a ride with us." Mm-hmm. We've
19 been together quite a while. *(He puts his paw on her*
20 *knee with a heavy thud. They sit for a moment. Alice*
21 *begins to sing tunelessly.)*
22 When Irish eyes are smiling
23 Oh it's like a summer day
24 But when Irish eyes are laughing
25 Oh it's like a big parade
26 *(During this, Sparky has begun to howl. Their voices*
27 *mingle. ALICE stops singing.)* Why, I guess you're
28 finished. *(Sparky rolls his eyes.)* You're a damn pig,
29 Sparky.
30
31
32
33
34
35

The Souvenir of Pompeii
by Sari Bodi

1 In *The Souvenir of Pompeii*, Sari Bodi presents the reaction of
2 a woman who learns that her neighbor has kidnapped a baby from
3 a hospital.
4
5
6 NATALIE: Yeah, I knew her. She was my next-door
7   neighbor, wasn't she? And I could have told you this
8   would happen, too. I knew she'd steal a baby. I would
9   have called the police if her husband hadn't. I could
10   see her staring at my four kids like she wished they
11   were hers. And just think, I let her hold my littlest
12   one, too. You know, just so she could get her
13   hormones flowing and have one of her own. But she's
14   the type that'll probably never have a kid. She's too
15   skinny. You gotta have some fat on you to produce
16   babies. That's a fact. Yeah, I knew she'd do something
17   like this. She read too much. Whenever I stopped over
18   her house to show her my kids, and let her touch them
19   and stuff, she'd be reading some book on ancient
20   civilizations. Then she'd tell me how women in Greek
21   society didn't have any status. I mean, who cares? She
22   should come to my house and see how much status I
23   got. But I could see how she felt like a failure. I mean
24   conceiving a kid is probably one of the easiest things
25   you'll ever do in your life. You know I'm sure she got
26   A's on all her papers in school, and I got C's, but hey
27   in the test on populating the universe, she's now
28   getting an F. Like I said, it never pays to be an over-
29   achiever. It's a much happier place in the middle. I
30   kept telling her, you want one of these babies like I

1 got, then stop reading those books and relax. I
2 mean I've only ever read three books all the way
3 through and look at all the kids I have. Number one
4 was *The Bridges of Madison County*, of course.
5 But you couldn't show your face at a Tupperware
6 party in this neighborhood if you hadn't read that.
7 Number two was *Women Who Love Too Much*,
8 well, cause that's me. But my absolute favorite is
9 still *Gone with the Wind*. Sometimes at night when
10 all the kids are sleeping, and Glen is snoring so I
11 really can't sleep, I'll pretend that this house is
12 Tara and that Glen has all his hair and is Rhett
13 Butler. You know, I don't tell my kids about this
14 Scarlett O'Hara stuff because I don't want them to
15 be encouraged by dreams. Dreams are very
16 harmful. I mean it's very unlikely — probably a
17 million to one chance of one of them becoming
18 president, so why give them false hopes. But
19 they're healthy kids. And you know why? It's
20 because I breast fed each one of them till they were
21 two years old. It was a sacrifice cause sometimes it
22 looked a little funny to have one of them walk up to
23 me and take a suck, but ... Hey, do you want to see
24 them? They're probably the healthiest kids you'll
25 ever see. Oh, okay, well then some other time. No,
26 I don't know where she is. I'm certainly not hiding
27 her here. I think a woman who takes a mother's
28 baby should be shot. She doesn't respect the birth
29 process. And I'd tell her that to her face. Well, I tell
30 you, when Glen and I were watching the television
31 last night and saw her picture on the news, it was
32 the most surprised I ever saw Glen. Well, we'd
33 never known a celebrity before. So Glen says to me,
34 "See I told you she was crazy." And of course he
35 never did but he always likes to be right about

1   people. So I said, "No, Glen, I told you she was
2   going crazy, but you never listen to me." And he
3   says, "No, I'm the one that spotted it." So we went
4   back and forth like this, until it suddenly came to
5   me. Here is a chance to use my all-time favorite
6   line, so I sat back in my chair, pushed my dinner
7   away, and said, "Frankly, my dear, I don't give a
8   damn." So I won the argument. Which I have to say
9   was one of the most fun moments of my marriage.
10
11
12
13
14
15
16
17
18
19
20
21
22
23
24
25
26
27
28
29
30
31
32
33
34
35

Telling Tales

by Migdalia Cruz

1 Migdalia Cruz's *Telling Tales* includes a series of character
2 sketches. "Papo Chibirico" was her first love.

Papo Chibirico

5 Papo Chibirico was fifteen when I was seven. He was
6 my first love. He bought me coloring books and candy
7 and took me to the zoo. Anthony Vargas tried to give
8 me coloring books too, but I punched him in the nose
9 and made him bleed. Papo thought it was a good idea.
10 "Don't let the boys bully you," he always said. Every
11 summer we formed softball teams. Once we were
12 playing and I walked backwards to make a catch. I
13 didn't know I was on a hill and fell off into a pile of
14 beer bottles. Papo carried me the fifteen blocks home
15 with one hand holding my left knee together. He
16 pulled the glass out of the wound and went with my
17 Mom and me to the hospital. He was mature for a kid.
18 That's what I thought. When I turned eleven, I went to
19 P.R. for the summer. I returned a foot and a half taller
20 and five shades darker. Papo was six inches shorter
21 than me then. How could he be six inches shorter, if
22 he was eight years older? Papo changed that summer
23 too, he got more muscles and was training to become
24 a wrestler. My dad and I watched his first televised
25 fight on channel forty-seven. That's when I found out
26 he was a midget—because he was a midget wrestler.
27 Papo fought the Jamaican Kid. The strength was in
28 their arms really. Their little legs just kicked the air.
29 With their arms they pinned each other to the floor.
30 My Dad laughed and I wondered what was so funny.

1   He explained to me that it was supposed to be
2   funny — that's why you watch midget wrestling, to
3   laugh. The Jamaican Kid won. The next day I saw
4   Papo. He was still friendly to me even though he
5   was a TV star. All the kids on the block wanted to
6   talk to him. But he talked just to me. The big kids
7   were always challenging him in a fight. He would
8   say "No," but they would push him and hit him until
9   there was nothing left to say. Sometimes three or
10   four would gang up on him and hold him up in the
11   air. His useless legs would swing wildly at his
12   attackers always missing their mark. "Some tough
13   guy!" Then they'd throw him into a dumpster. I
14   used to watch and cry because I didn't know what
15   else to do. All I could do was wait for them to leave
16   and help Papo out of the garbage. He always got
17   mad at me then. "Don't you know you could get
18   hurt?! Stay away from me, will you! I don't need
19   your help!" But he always needed my help. He got
20   to be a really good wrestler. The kind the crowd
21   stands up for. He got tougher too. Carried a knife
22   and stabbed somebody, so I couldn't see him
23   anymore. He'd look at me from across the street
24   when I was sitting on the fire escape doing my
25   homework. He waved and I waved back, but he
26   always turned away before he saw me wave. I guess
27   he was afraid I wouldn't. When he got a little money
28   saved, he got a special bicycle on which he could
29   reach the pedals. He spent hours on that bike,
30   circling the neighborhood. I watched him go by and
31   go by and go by again. He looked normal on that
32   bike — happy. He walked with a limp now. The
33   Jamaican Kid went crazy one night and bit a chunk
34   out of his calf. He got an infection from it. The
35   Jamaican Kid never even apologized. I know

because I asked. That's the last thing we ever talked about. It was one of those real hot August nights, when everybody's on the street because nobody can sleep. Some guys are playing the congas in the playground, small children are playing tag, mothers are gossiping and the men are playing dominoes. Papo comes by on his bike. It's a pretty one — black with a red seat and Papo's in red and black too. He looks sharp. His face is pretty. He's the only one on the block with green eyes. Everybody wanted those eyes. Everybody says hello. He starts showing off, making the bike jump and taking turns real fast and low. People applaud. He does this over and over, people finally stop watching but he keeps saying "Look at me, look at me!" Now people are embarrassed to look. Papo goes by one more time ... I don't know where the car came from. It was a new car, I think. Shiny. Maybe just freshly waxed. People always wax their cars in the summer. He wouldn't have lived long anyway — that's what people said. "God bless him. Midgets don't live very long." But he wasn't a midget, he was a dwarf.

Still Blooming
by Jane Hill

1   The following selection of *Still Blooming* by Jane Hill contains
2 the remembrances of an elderly woman.
3
4
5 **SHIRLEY: Good afternoon. I'm Shirley Wrinkle. The**
6   **world's oldest living tap dancer, I'm one hundred and**
7   **three.** *(Pause)* **All right. One hundred and ten. The**
8   **world forgives a woman for lying about her age.**
9   **Awright, awright. I'm only ninety-two. But nobody's**
10   **interested in an old woman unless she's over a**
11   **hundred. Not even Willard Scott. I want to thank Mrs.**
12   **Moore, the chairman of your entertainment**
13   **committee, for inviting me here today to share some**
14   **reflections about my long and fascinating life. And I'm**
15   **going to let you in on a few important secrets I've**
16   **discovered. For example, some of you have already**
17   **noticed I use a walker. There are two ways to look at**
18   **a walker. If there are any "New Age" types here, it's**
19   **kind of like the "half-empty/half-full" glass analogy.**
20   **Well, never mind. The walker. Two ways to look at it.**
21   **You can see it as a sign of your physical deterioration.**
22   **Or you can see it for what it really is. An opportunity**
23   **for four more tap shoes. Please don't think I'm being**
24   **brave. Crap, no! I'm being realistic.** *(Looks around*
25   *cautiously and waves sweetly to someone in the audience.)*
26   **Sorry, Estelle. I forgot and used the "C" word. Estelle**
27   **brought me here in the hospital van. She's on the**
28   **staff. For "By-the-Sea Convalescent Care Home."**
29   **Practically overlooks the Pacific, if you can see that**
30   **far. It's a lovely place. Charming. No, really. Of**

1course, the residents call it the "Bide-a-Wee." Why?
2Because no one expects to stay long. And yet no
3one actually believes they'll die, do they? Oops,
4now I did it. I used the "D" word. But I didn't mean
5to digress. You aren't here to listen to my views of
6death. I have two areas of expertise. Two reasons
7why the "Bide-a-Wee" management takes me on
8these little jaunts to share my gifts with the general
9public. I am, as I stated, the world's oldest living
10tap dancer. But I also know a lot about romance.
11That's a hot topic these days. What exactly is
12romance, you wonder? It's the Yuppie version of
13love. The cleaned-up version of sex. And I've spent
14many years reflecting on it. I've been in love. The
15first time I was seventeen. The last time — let me
16amend that — the most *recent* time, I was eighty-
17three. He was a beast. All he thought about was
18sex, sex, sex. You look confused, madam. Do I
19mean seventeen or eighty-three? Both! Yes, it's a
20popular misconception that the elderly are not
21interested in sex any more. Don't you believe it. It
22causes a lot of problems at the "Bide-a-Wee."
23Romance blooms, but it's nipped in the bud by
24Sominex. I've been married six times. Well, you
25don't get to be an expert without a lot of research,
26I always say. I married for love each time. My first
27husband, Alfredo, was a performer with an Italian
28circus. There's something about a man in spangled
29tights that's just irresistible. I grew up in a small
30town in western Pennsylvania. One of those dreary
31coal mining towns, you know? But I always knew I
32was destined for a career in show business. The
33week the circus stayed in our town I attended every
34performance. By the end of the week, I knew every
35routine by heart. Alfredo's act was the most

exciting. He was shot out of a real cannon. No
mirror tricks, you know! Boom! And off he went. It
was thrilling. I always ran out to see where he
landed. Always the same spot. This pile of foam
padding. He never missed. Well, once. But that's
another part of my story. You see, when the circus
left town, I went with them. By then I was
completely smitten. And within two months,
Alfredo and I were married. I soon became part of
the show, helping with the act. My job — in a
glamorous costume, of course — was to load the
cannon with the exact amount of powder required.
And then, on an exciting musical crescendo, to
touch a torch to the charge. I learned just how to
build the suspense. For a year, we were happy as
two little pigeons. And then I discovered Alfredo
was unfaithful. In fact, he had several other wives
in the small towns on our tour circuit. That's when
the accident happened. One night something went
wrong with the powder charge. There was a huge
explosion and Alfredo sailed into the night sky. I
remember there was a full moon ... his spangled
tights glittering and glistening, his beautiful body
silhouetted against the moon. He never did come
down. Or at least we never discovered where. It
was a spectacular finish to the act, of course.
Personally, I think Alfredo was lucky. He didn't
outlast our love. Each time I've been in love, I've
had a similar reaction. A sort of death wish. Now
that's not cynical. It's realistic. Because we live in
the nineties, for Gods sake. We've screwed up just
about everything. The air. The water. The rain
forest. So you tell me ... You're in love, the most
sublime of states. What do you wish for? The end
of the world, if you're smart. Who in their right

1   mind would want to survive love? And romance?
2   Ah, romance! Unlike love, romance lasts. Romance
3   is the residue of love. *(Spotting a particular audience*
4   *member)* Ah, I saw that smile. You know what I'm
5   talking about. Well, I won't betray you. We
6   romantics have to stick together. When people find
7   out about us, they won't leave us alone. They feel
8   compelled to cry and "burst the bubble." Keep
9   trying to convince you that the actual experience
10   was better than the memory. What nonsense! Our
11   only defense is to pretend we're senile. Just don't
12   listen. Take up crafts. Knitting is good. Look
13   carefully at the next knitter you see. They usually
14   have a little smile on their face. Knit one, purl two.
15   *(She demonstrates the tiny smile of the "secret*
16   *romantic.")* Sure sign of a romantic. And contrary to
17   popular opinion, most of us elderly romantics are
18   not clinging desperately to life. Or this shabby
19   substitute for it that's known as "old age." I once
20   had a dear friend at the "Bide-a-Wee," Eunice
21   Wilson. She was in terrible shape. Lots of pain. One
22   day she said to me, "Shirley, I just don't get it. I've
23   cleaned up all the odds and ends of my life. I seem
24   to be just hanging around here, taking up space.
25   Why can't I die?" Well, as a matter of fact, this
26   particular woman was quite a resource for
27   everyone else at the "Bide-a-Wee." She was sharp
28   as a tack. Anyhow, in her day, Eunice had been a
29   great gardener. And she liked to be turned in her
30   bed so she could look out at this little plot of
31   flowers next to the hospital. So, a few days later, I
32   shuffled in to see her. She was in her usual
33   position, gazing out the window. She said, "Shirley,
34   I've figured out why I can't die yet. I'm still
35   blooming." *(Notices Estelle again.)* Well, I see that

1   **Estelle is giving me the high sign, so it's time for**
2   **my number. Hit it, Estelle.** *(Piano intro begins to the*
3   *tune of "Tea for Two." Follow spot comes on, if*
4   *available.)*
5   **Picture me, the "Bide-a-Wee"**
6   **Just tea for one and one for tea**
7   **Just me myself, just me with me alone.**
8   **Nobody near me to see me or hear me,**
9   **No friends or relations on weekend vacations,**
10   **I won't have it known, dear,**
11   **That I can't afford a phone, dear.**
12   **Day will break and I'll awake,**
13   **My joints may ache**
14   **But still I'll make**
15   **An effort to have fun, to still be me!**
16   **I've outlived my family,**
17   **But I've no time for misery,**
18   **Can't you see what's bloomin' here is me?!**
19   *(Dance break. SHIRLEY executes a halting tap dance*
20   *routine with her own tap shoes and those of the walker.)*
21   **I've outlived my family,**
22   **But I've no time for misery,**
23   **Can't you see what's bloomin' here — it's me!**
24   *(Takes her bows, then begins waving to Estelle.)* **That's**
25   **right, Estelle, you get the van warmed up while I**
26   **say goodnight to the nice people. Sssshhh!**
27   **Sssshhh! I got to talk fast here. I don't know crap**
28   **about tap dancing. You got all nostalgic, because**
29   **you thought my aged infirmities had diminished my**
30   **abilities. Baloney! I only started studying this stuff**
31   **six months ago. When I got the walker! It was an**
32   **inspired idea — my ticket out of the "Bide-a-Wee"**
33   **a couple of times a month. I took the med-car.**
34   **Everyone thought I was going to the doctor, but I**
35   **scooted around the corner to my tap teacher. Well,**

1   I'm not ashamed to be a subversive. As a tap
2   dancer I confess I'm a fake. A fraud. A beginner.
3   But I've always wanted to do it. You know what it
4   is for me? And this is the real secret I came here to
5   share with you. It's a fierce embrace of physicality.
6   So what if it's only from the ankles down! Don't let
7   anybody talk you into giving that up. Get the
8   message. Keep blooming! *(Song reprise without piano*
9   *accompaniment or follow spot)*
10   I've outlived my family,
11   But I've no time for misery.
12   Can't you see what's bloomin' here — that's me!
13
14
15
16
17
18
19
20
21
22
23
24
25
26
27
28
29
30
31
32
33
34
35

Scenes for
One Male

Wicked Games
by Paul Boakye

1   In *Wicked Games*, Paul Boake explores a thirty-four-year-old
2 black man's concern that both men and women misinterpret his
3 romantic interests.

4

5

6 **LEO: People always think because I'm friendly, I'm flirting.**
7   **Or I'm into them sexually. With my best friend Mark**
8   **when he went mad, and it literally happened like that.**
9   *(Snaps fingers.)* **I was there. I had a hard time with him**
10   **and it shattered the beliefs I had in our friendship. I**
11   **still stuck by him. And now he's out of hospital he**
12   **doesn't remember that day. He doesn't remember**
13   **anything he said. Or did, and I've just got to blank it**
14   **out myself. I still think hard about what I say to him.**
15   **Try not to upset him. Make sure I'm not being more**
16   **physical to his girlfriend Tina than he thinks I should**
17   **be. Or that I'm giving her more attention or whatever.**
18   **Although Tina was my friend before he was. We were**
19   **lovers twelve years ago. But he came into the eternal**
20   **triangle six years ago ... and it worries him that she'll**
21   **always take my side — except where he comes first.**
22   **But I think that's a mean way of thinking. When I met**
23   **him he was doing nothing. I sorted him out. Got him**
24   **a flat in Holland Park. Introduced him to Tina, but he**
25   **just feels there's part of her that he can't have. But**
26   **that's true of everyone though. I mean, the way you**
27   **talk to people never mirrors what you're really**
28   **thinking inside.**

29

30

Infrared

by Mac Wellman

1   In this selection from Mac Wellman's *Infrared*, the narrator
2 considers what he has to learn about the nature of his life.
3
4
5 **NARRATOR: All this seems so strangely familiar to me. All**
6   **this I know, as if by** *deja vu.* **from some other world**
7   **linked to this one by time's worm-hole, and there is so**
8   **much I want to learn. So much to learn. Before ...**
9   **before they come for me, as I am certain they will.**
10   **Because of the shadow, the shadow that was not mine**
11   **that I brought with me all the way from the world of**
12   **Infrared ...** *(In truth, the Shadow is acting like a bag full of*
13   *schizophrenic alley cats. An ominous black sedan pulls up.*
14   *The sedan is filled with dark red light. Two men dressed in*
15   *black get out. They both carry blackjacks and are masked.*
16   *Our NARRATOR doesn't see them but his shadow does and*
17   *quakes with fear.)* **I want to learn why a thing can**
18   **resemble another thing, but not be at all the same; I**
19   **want to know where our dreams come from, and how**
20   **it is possible for us to desire things that injure us, or**
21   **drive us mad; I want to know what the true limits of the**
22   **human condition are — and how we are to know when**
23   **we have gone too far — when we have disappeared into**
24   **the hole of our own undoing; I want to know why I have**
25   **become so disfigured that I cannot bear my own image,**
26   **and even my own shadow is a visual horror to me; I**
27   **want to know what love is, and why when you reach to**
28   **hold it, it flies off in terror like the uncaged paroquet,**
29   **confused by sudden freedom; I want so badly to know**
30   **why oh why is there anything at all ...**

Barking Sharks
by Israel Horovitz

1   Israel Horovitz's first highly acclaimed play, *Park Your Car in*
2   *Harvard Yard*, was followed by numerous theatrical and cinematic
3   offerings, many of which were set in New England. In this selection
4   from *Barking Sharks*, a middle-aged businessman observes that his
5   son's actions reflect his own actions.
6
7
8   **RALPH BURKE: Nothing gives me pleasure. My first wife's**
9   **dead. My second wife's re-married. None of my kids**
10   **give a damn about me. They probably do, on some**
11   **level. I mean, they probably talk about me in their**
12   **psychoanalytic sessions, right? But, they don't ever,**
13   **like, *call* me ... I mean, they don't actually wanna *see***
14   **me. And, to tell you the God's honest truth, I don't**
15   **really know, deep down, if I actually wanna see *them*!**
16   **It's a terrible thing to say out loud, isn't it? I know, at**
17   **my age, you're s'posed ta love takin' walks with your**
18   **grandchildren, but, I don't, I really don't! I know**
19   **they're just kids, and I should be generous with them**
20   **and all, but, honest ta God, they're not nice people.**
21
22   . . .
23   **My whole family. Selfish, money-grubbing, nasty to**
24   **each other, whiney, endless bickering ... My son's a**
25   **lousy husband and father, big-time. He's screwing**
26   **anything that wears a skirt.**
27
28   . . .
29   **It's obvious! I know what he's doin', 'cause he learned**
30   **it from me! He acts like a piece of shit to his kids, and**

1   **it makes me hate myself!** *(BURKE's emotions are over*
2   *the top. He grabs a presentation notebook from the*
3   *tabletop and flings it down on the floor, angrily.)*
4
5
6
7
8
9
10
11
12
13
14
15
16
17
18
19
20
21
22
23
24
25
26
27
28
29
30
31
32
33
34
35

Double or Nothing
by Michael Ajakwe, Jr.

1   Frank, a twenty-eight-year-old, blue-collar African-American
2 remembers meeting a woman whom he now loves in this selection
3 from Michael Ajakwe, Jr.'s *Double or Nothing*.
4
5
6 **FRANK:** *(Singing)* **"Love them and leave them ... That's**
7   **what I used to to ... use and abuse them ..."** *(Beat;*
8   *normal speak)* **Until I met Sherry.** *(Savoring the memory)*
9   **I'll never forget it.** *(Lights fade to dim. Music fades up low*
10   *under. It's 2nd Nature's "Base Tone Junkies." At the bar,*
11   *on the other side of the room, a gorgeous woman,*
12   *SHERRY, 29, is staring at what is now a packed dance*
13   *floor, nursing a drink and watching the festivities.)* **She**
14   **was just sitting there, all by her lonesome, having**
15   **what looked like a Screaming Orgasm but could've**
16   **just as well been a V-8. Now, normally, it ain't my**
17   **style to ask a babe to dance, 'specially when she's**
18   **thirty feet away, 'cause if I do and she says no**
19   **everybody in the house is gonna know about** *(A guy*
20   *moves from across the room to ask SHERRY to dance. She*
21   *stares him up and down like he's a Martian, shakes her*
22   *head and looks away, leaving him standing there in front*
23   *of the whole room like an idiot. The guy looks at the*
24   *audience, embarrassed, and attempts to "casually" ease*
25   *Off-stage.)* **See. That could've been me — an accident**
26   **waiting to happen.** *(SHERRY makes eye contact with*
27   *FRANK. FRANK looks around, unsure whether she's*
28   *actually looking at him. He points to himself and she nods,*
29   *looking away.)* **Ya'll see that! Got her cold busied. And**
30   **she didn't even try to hide it.** *(Beat)* **Women ... Ya'll**

1   think ya'll so slick. And you are. But one thing's for
2   sure — when you wanna let a brother know what
3   time it is, ya'll don't waste no time. *(Beat)* So, what
4   do ya'll think? Should I "go for it?" Should I "make
5   my move?" Or should I just straight up "bum-rush
6   the show?"*(Off their looks)* That means everything I
7   just said. *(To a confused patron)* What's the matter,
8   ain't never lived in the ghetto before? Didn't think
9   so. *(Beat, setting his sights back on SHERRY)* I think
10   I'm gonna go for it. *(Starts for the bar, then stops.)* But
11   if she turns me down, I'm kicking somebody's ass.
12
13
14
15
16
17
18
19
20
21
22
23
24
25
26
27
28
29
30
31
32
33
34
35

Cheap Sentiment

by Bruce Graham

1   Screenwriting is the subject of a dramatic diatribe by an exiled
2   author in Bruce Graham's *Cheap Sentiment*: "During the
3   communist witch hunt of the 1950s, Giddy fled Tinseltown for an
4   obscure life fishing for crabs on the Chesapeake. Nearly thirty years
5   later, he is discovered by an idealistic young director who becomes
6   determined to make Giddy's unfinished masterpiece into a motion
7   picture. Here, two very different generations of filmmakers clash as
8   Giddy reacts to the younger man's sense of style.
9
10
11 **GIDDY: Damn, it's been a long time. Last movie I went ta**
12   **see was *The French Connection*. Thought it was**
13   **gonna' be a girlie flick.** *(Back to DAVID as he moves to*
14   *the Victrola.)* **You get what I'm sayin', right? When**
15   **people go to all that trouble and spend all that money**
16   **they wanta' feel good when they walk out.** *(Music*
17   *begins: "Sonny Boy.")* **Listen to that. Talk about your**
18   **cheap sentiment — Jesus Christ, Jolson was the**
19   **master. But my uncle, who was one tough sonuvabitch**
20   **— I saw him take on three of Capone's guys with a**
21   **meat cleaver in one hand and a pork roast in the other**
22   **— he bawled his eyes out when he heard that song.**
23   **Why? — did he care about the kid in the song —**
24   **Christ no. Like most people, he had a crappy life. He**
25   **hated the meat business, he hated my aunt — what a**
26   **heifer she was, shoulda butchered her. But when we**
27   **came outta that Jolson show ... he had laughed, he**
28   **had cried ... and I'd never seen him so happy in his**
29   **life. And even though Jolson was a bastard, we loved**
30   **him. That's why she's gotta' fall in the water. We take**

1　this cold bitch in the first five minutes — she gets
2　in a jam — boom — falls in the water — she makes
3　us laugh. Now she's human, we start ta like her.
4　Then we care about her. Then we like the
5　goddamned movie and we tell all our friends to go
6　see it and make a lotta money! *(Em crosses through*
7　*the yard, all dressed up.)* Nobody goes to a movie
8　cause of the goddamned "thematic underpinnings."
9　Basic primal emotions, Dave, that's why! Emotions!
10　*(With passion; he sounds more like Irv than GIDDY.)* We
11　all have 'em. And if you touch that in your audience
12　— that's our job: make 'em laugh, make 'em cry —
13　then you've done something good.
14
15
16
17
18
19
20
21
22
23
24
25
26
27
28
29
30
31
32
33
34
35

Brothers

by William Gadea

1   Years ago, Biff, a man in his thirties, caused his younger brother
2   to lose his head, literally. In William Gadea's *Brothers*, this event is
3   recounted.
4
5
6   **BIFF:** *(As himself)* **Hold it there, Lorraine! I think I can**
7   **answer that question.** *(RAY rolls his eyes and crosses his*
8   *arms disgustedly. As BIFF drifts into the reverie of memory*
9   *a light isolates him; the sounds of the scene he describes*
10   *can be heard.)* **Many years ago Ray and me were two**
11   **perfectly normal kids growing up in the American**
12   **heartland. Every morning before school our Mama**
13   **would kiss us goodbye, and every morning she'd say**
14   **to me: "Look after your brother, Biff. Now that your**
15   **Dad is gone you have to look out for him." Porky was**
16   **the bully of my grade. One day at lunchtime he was**
17   **pushing me around like usual ... when a ball came**
18   **bouncing between us. And who should come running**
19   **after it? My little brother Ray. Laughing, Porky and**
20   **his friends grabbed Ray and carried him away. I tried**
21   **to get them to stop but ... there were too many of**
22   **them. Before I knew it they were screwing him head**
23   **first into a drain-hole behind the gym. I yelled "stop,**
24   **stop!" but they wouldn't stop. They wouldn't stop**
25   **until his head was stuck in the drain-hole up to his**
26   **shoulders. I was crying! I didn't know what to do. I**
27   **should have called for help, but all I could think about**
28   **was getting him out. I didn't know any better. I pulled**
29   **him by his ankles! I pulled and pulled as hard as I**
30   **could and then: I heard a pop. Like champagne being**

1   uncorked. And I heard his head ... as it rolled down
2   the drain. Down the drain ... and out of our lives
3   forever. It is true — I have failed Ray. There's
4   nothing I can do to give him his head back. But I
5   can try to make up for it! And I will! And — he
6   always cries when I get to this part — *(RAY's*
7   *shoulders are shaking, but only because he's laughing.)*
8   I'm going to do everything in my power to give him
9   a normal life. My little brother is going to have
10   everything an ordinary guy would have — a place to
11   live, hobbies, a TV — yes, even a girlfriend! That
12   much I have promised him, and that much will I do
13   for him. That's pretty much the long and the short
14   of it.
15
16
17
18
19
20
21
22
23
24
25
26
27
28
29
30
31
32
33
34
35

Molly Sweeny

by Brian Friel

1   One of Ireland's leading contemporary dramatists, Brian Friel
2 gained an international reputation in 1990 with *Dancing at*
3 *Lughnasa* which won the 1992 Tony Award for best play. *Molly*
4 *Sweeny* includes Frank's recollection of the first time that he asked
5 Molly to go out with him.

6

7

8 **FRANK: I spent a week in the library — the week after I**
9   **first met her — one full week immersing myself in**
10   **books and encyclopedias and magazines and articles**
11   **— anything, everything I could find about eyes and**
12   **vision and eye diseases and blindness. Fascinating. I**
13   **can't tell you — fascinating. I look out of my bedroom**
14   **window and at a single glance I see the front garden**
15   **and the road beyond and cars and buses and the**
16   **tennis courts on the far side and people playing on**
17   **them and the hills beyond that. Everything — all those**
18   **details and dozens more — all seen in one immediate,**
19   **comprehensive perception. But Molly's world isn't**
20   **perceived instantly, comprehensively. She composes**
21   **a world from a sequence of impressions; one after the**
22   **other, in time. For example, she knows that this is a**
23   **carving knife because first she can feel the handle:**
24   **then she can feel this long blade: then this sharp edge.**
25   **In sequence. In time. What is this object? These are**
26   **ears. This is a furry body. Those are paws. That is a**
27   **long tail. Ah, a cat! In sequence. Sequentially. Right?**
28   **Right. Now a personal question. You are going to ask**
29   **this blind lady out for an evening. What would be the**
30   **ideal entertainment for somebody like her? A meal? A**

1   concert? A walk? Maybe a swim? Billy Hughes says
2   she's a wonderful swimmer. *(He shakes his head*
3   *slowly.)* The week in the library pays off. Know the
4   answer instantly. Dancing. Take her dancing. With
5   her disability the perfect, the absolutely perfect
6   relaxation. Forget about space, distance, who's
7   close, who's far, who's approaching. Forget about
8   time. This is not a sequence of events. This is one
9   continuous, delightful event. Nothing leads to
10   nothing else. There is only now. There is nothing
11   subsequent. I am your eyes, your ears, your
12   location, your sense of space. Trust me. Dancing.
13   Obvious. Straight into a phone-box and asked her
14   would she come with me to the Hikers Club dance
15   the following Saturday. It'll be small, I said; more
16   like a party. What do you say? Silence. We'll ask
17   Billy and Rita and we'll make it a foursome and
18   we'll have our own table and our own fun. Not a
19   word. Please, Molly. In my heart of hearts I really
20   didn't think she'd say yes. For God's sake why
21   should she? Middle-aged. No skill. No job. No
22   prospect of a job. Two rooms above Kelly's cake
23   shop. And not exactly Rudolf Valentino. And when
24   she did speak, when she said very politely, "Thank
25   you, Frank. I'd love to go," do you know what I
26   said? "All right then." Bloody brilliant! But I vowed
27   to myself in that phone-box, I made a vow there
28   and then that at the dance on Saturday night I
29   wouldn't open the big mouth — big? — enormous
30   for Christ's sake! — I wouldn't open it once all
31   night, all week. Talking of Valentino, in point of fact
32   Valentino was no Adonis himself. Average height;
33   average looks; mediocre talent. And if he hadn't
34   died so young — in 1926 — he was only thirty-one
35   — and in those mysterious circumstances that were

1 never fully explained — he would never have
2 become the cult figure the studios worked so hard
3 to ... Anyhow ...
4
5
6
7
8
9
10
11
12
13
14
15
16
17
18
19
20
21
22
23
24
25
26
27
28
29
30
31
32
33
34
35

Happy Anniversary, Punk!

by Michael Ajakwe, Jr.

1   A man plans revenge for his son's murder in Michael Ajakwe,

2 Jr.'s *Happy Anniversary, Punk!*

3

4

5 **AL: Damn! One hundred-fourteen million, eight hundred-**

6   **forty thousand seconds. One million, nine hundred-**

7   **fourteen thousand minutes. Twenty-one thousand,**

8   **nine hundred hours. Three hundred sixty-five days.**

9   **Fifty-two weeks. Twelve months. I can't believe it's**

10   **been a year.** *(Beat)* **I remember it like it was yesterday.**

11   **I was at the post office, preparing for my annual**

12   **review. The phone rings. I assume it's my wife, calling**

13   **to find out if I got promoted. I'm right. It's her.** *(Beat)*

14   **Our son had been shot on his way home from school.**

15   **She was at the hospital. By the time I got there he was**

16   **gone.** *(Beat)* **Randall. Randall Bean-Fletcher. I wanted**

17   **to name him Al after me. But making a boy go**

18   **through life being called by another man's name just**

19   **didn't seem right to me. Sure I had to do it. But I**

20   **didn't have a choice. What can a newborn say when**

21   **his daddy names him "Junior?" "Feed me!" That's**

22   **about it. So when I became a daddy I decided to play**

23   **God and change the rules.** *(Beat)* **Most fathers would**

24   **spend a day like this at the cemetery or picketing in**

25   **front of the courthouse, demanding a retrial. My**

26   **wife's at the cemetery right now with her mother. Not**

27   **me. Cemeteries are like all other rituals of death —**

28   **they're for the living. The dead don't care. Hell,**

29   **they're dead. Besides, I'm tired of crying. Nope. Ain't**

30   **gonna be no more tears coming out of these eyes. No,**

1   sir! I'm a man, goddamnit! Leave the whimpering
2   and whining to the women and children. Real men
3   don't cry — they get even. *(Beat)* The kid who killed
4   Randall was a year younger than him. Only fifteen
5   years old. They caught him, locked him up for nine
6   months, then let him out. Said he was no longer a
7   "danger to society." Said he was "reformed."
8   Sometimes, when I'm watering the lawn, I see him
9   drive by my house in his mama's Honda, seat
10   cocked back pimp-daddy style, lookin' like Snoop
11   Hot Diggity Damn Dog. He don't say nothin', but I
12   can hear him loud and clear: "I'm free! I'm free!
13   And ain't nothin' you can do to me, old dude. Be
14   cool." *(Beat)* Kids can be so stupid. They think just
15   because you're grown you gotta be responsible all
16   the time. Do the right thing; that you can't just nut
17   up and go crazy, like them. Well, today, I'm
18   pleading "temporary insanity."
19
20
21
22
23
24
25
26
27
28
29
30
31
32
33
34
35

The Souvenir of Pompeii
by Sari Bodi

1   In *The Souvenir of Pompeii*, Sari Bodi presents the dilemma
2 of a man whose wife has kidnapped a baby from a hospital.
3
4
5   **SAM: I don't know where Helen is. I'm not hiding her. I**
6   **wouldn't keep a baby that wasn't mine. I'm too**
7   **honest. I was brought up to believe that if I worked**
8   **hard, was nice to my neighbors, and gave money to**
9   **charity, my life would run smoothly. Just this morning**
10   **when I was at the supermarket, a woman asked me to**
11   **feed the homeless. Which I did, literally. You actually**
12   **slip your money into the mouth of a plastic homeless**
13   **person. It was a bit off-putting at first, but actually**
14   **quite satisfying. And I thought that that act would put**
15   **me in good stead with the Fates. But it didn't.**
16   **Because when I got back from the supermarket, Helen**
17   **is sitting in the kitchen trying to feed milk to a baby.**
18   **"This is Pericles," she says. "The child we created last**
19   **night." And she is so convinced, that for a split second**
20   **I wonder if I remembered to buy baby food. "Helen,**
21   **this is not our baby," I say. The baby starts to scream.**
22   **"We need to find its mother, Helen. Where did you get**
23   **her? Do I have to call the police?" "You want to give**
24   **your child to the police?" she says. "How silly. Sam.**
25   **After all the time we've spent trying to create her." I**
26   **do want a child. When we were first married, Helen**
27   **and I would imagine ourselves as a mother hen and a**
28   **rooster with a brood of chicks following us wherever**
29   **we went. But now when I see the children on the block**
30   **running after the ice cream truck, I imagine that the**

1   Good Humor man is the Pied Piper who will pack
2   them all up in the truck, and unfreeze them only
3   after I am dead. Helen thinks her fertility problem
4   stems from a prehistoric biological problem. That a
5   woman in the cave days who had her high level of
6   anxiety would have been prevented from releasing
7   eggs because it meant that wild animals were
8   nearby which might devour the newborn. But she
9   has a new historical theory every month. And none
10 of them work. And do you know why? Because
11 Helen and I have bad luck. That's all it is. Bad luck.
12 And there is nothing you can do about that. Not
13 even steal a baby. Which is probably the worst
14 crime anyone could commit. And I tell Helen this
15 while the baby is screaming. Which probably wasn't
16 the right thing to do because Helen grabbed the
17 baby and ran. I was left holding the milk carton. I
18 had to call the police. And well, here you are. You
19 probably have children of your own, don't you?
20 You'll leave here, and go home to a house full of
21 screaming kids. Wonderfully screaming kids. And
22 we'll be left here — with the quiet.
23
24
25
26
27
28
29
30
31
32
33
34
35

Dead or Alive

by Karen Smith Vastola

1   Karen Smith Vastola's Seth, a forty-year-old man in the mood
2 for love, finds panty hose a hindrance to his mood in this selection
3 from *Dead or Alive*.

4

5

6 **SETH: Whoever invented those things must have been a**
7   **man-hater.**

8

9   **...**

10   **Put yourself in a man's shoe or some other place.**
11   **You have a date with a woman. A woman you really**
12   **like, or maybe not. A woman you really have had the**
13   **hots for a long time, or maybe you just have the hots.**
14   **I mean the horns are on. You take her to the movies**
15   **or the theatre if she thinks of herself as one of the**
16   **more cultivated types. You have drinks and dinner**
17   **before. You have drinks afterward. Now you've**
18   **invested two hundred or more for the privilege of this**
19   **woman's company. You're back at her apartment and**
20   **you do more talking. You listen attentively, patiently**
21   **to everything she's had to say, even the nonsense**
22   **about her number and your number and how**
23   **numerlogically speaking you're not quite a match.**
24   **You've bitten your lower lip until it's almost bled as**
25   **you try to hold back your laughter at her description**
26   **of her own personal angel that will accompany her**
27   **into the next millennium. You finally have her trust.**
28   **You try the kiss. It leads to more. Before long you're**
29   **both entangled. The room echoes with sucking noises,**
30   **short, panting breaths, popping buttons. You've**

1   managed to disentangle her from most of her
2   clothing. You've even managed to disrobe yourself
3   without missing a beat or losing the upward spiral
4   of both of your passions, and then, the final
5   obstacle, her pantyhose. A synthetic blend so
6   tightly woven that trying to grab it and pull with
7   your fingers becomes a lesson in smooth surface
8   tension and the absence of traction. And God forbid
9   you try to poke a finger through it and rip it. You'll
10   only end up sending the woman screaming as she
11   rushes off the sofa, towards her medicine cabinet
12   to find a bottle of clear nail polish to "Stop the
13   run." So you try from the top down, but as you
14   fumble with the tight elastic around the waist you
15   realize it's quite possible these pantyhose may be
16   vacuum sealed. And if the woman is at all vain
17   about a little protruding belly and she's chosen the
18   control-top version you're dead in the water. You
19   might as well be stranded on a desert island with a
20   can of sardines and no key.

21
22   **MARGERY:** *(Interrupts speech.)* **Why don't you just ask her**
23   **to take them off?]**

24   **SETH: And admit defeat. Never. A yard to the goal line**
25   **and you ask the woman, the opposing team to carry**
26   **the ball. To the touchdown! Why, if the seduction**
27   **can't be complete a man's better off removing**
28   **himself from the situation, getting dressed and**
29   **regrouping until a better day, a summer day. Sans**
30   **pantyhose.**

31
32
33
34
35

Angels in America
by Tony Krushner

1   Tony Kushner's trilogy *Angels in America: Millennium*
2   *Approaches* premiered in 1991 and won the Pulitzer Prize in
3   1993. It is about gay life in the United States.
4
5
6   **SCENE:** *The last days of October. Rabbi Isidor Chemelwitz*
7   *alone onstage with a small coffin. It is a rough pine box*
8   *with two wooden pegs, one at the foot and one at the head,*
9   *holding the lid in place. A prayer shawl embroidered with*
10   *a Star of David is draped over the lid, and by the head a*
11   *yarzheit candle is burning.*
12   **RABBI ISIDOR CHEMELWITZ:** *(He speaks sonorously, with a*
13   *heavy Eastern European accent, unapologetically*
14   *consulting a sheet of notes for the family names.)* **Hello**
15   **and good morning. I am Rabbi Isidor Chemelwitz of**
16   **the Bronx Home for Aged Hebrews. We are here this**
17   **morning to pay respects at the passing of Sarah**
18   **Ironson, devoted wife of Benjamin Ironson, also**
19   **deceased, loving and caring mother of her sons**
20   **Morris, Abraham, and Samuel, and her daughters**
21   **Esther and Rachel; beloved grandmother of Max,**
22   **Mark, Louis, Lisa, Maria ... uh ... Lesley, Angela,**
23   **Doris, Luke and Eric.** *(Looks more closely at paper.)* **Eric?**
24   **This is a Jewish name?** *(Shrugs.)* **Eric. A large and**
25   **loving family. We assemble that we may mourn**
26   **collectively this good and righteous woman.** *(He looks*
27   *at the coffin.)*
28   **This woman. I did not know this woman. I cannot**
29   **accurately describe her attributes, nor do justice to**
30   **her dimensions. She was ... Well, in the Bronx Home**

1   for Aged Hebrews are many like this, the old, and
2   to many I speak but not to be frank with this one.
3   She preferred silence. So I do not know her and yet
4   I know her. She was ... *(He touches the coffin.)* ... not
5   a person but a whole kind of person, the ones who
6   crossed the ocean, who brought with us to America
7   the villages of Russia and Lithuania — and how we
8   struggled, and how we fought, for the family, for
9   the Jewish home, so that you would not grow up
10   here, in this strange place, in the melting pot where
11   nothing melted. Descendants of this immigrant
12   woman, you do not grow up in America, you and
13   your children and their children with the goyische
14   names. You do not live in America. No such place
15   exists. Your clay is the clay of some Litvak *shtetl,*
16   your air the air of the steppes — because she
17   carried the old world on her back across the ocean,
18   in a boat, and she put it down on Grand Concourse
19   Avenue, or in Flatbush, and she worked that earth
20   into your bones, and you pass it to your children,
21   this ancient, ancient culture and home. *(Little pause)*
22   You can never make that crossing that she made,
23   for such Great Voyages in this world do not any
24   more exist. But every day of your lives the miles
25   that voyage between that place and this one you
26   cross. Every day. You understand me? In you that
27   journey is.
28   So ...
29   She was the last of the Mohicans, this one was.
30   Pretty soon ... all the old will be dead.
31
32
33
34
35

Event Horizon
by Christopher Kyle

1   *Event Horizon*, by Christopher Kyle, contains the following
2   segment in which a father telephones his son to tell him that he has
3   been fired.
4
5
6   **MITCH: I lost my job.**
7   ...
8   **The firm is looking to build a multicultural**
9   **workplace and I guess I'm kind of a monocultural guy.**
10   ...
11   **Twenty years in that place and I'm out on my ass. I**
12   **was a rainmaker, for Christ's sake.**
13   ...
14   **It meant everything to me. I gave up my chance at**
15   **a family life for those bastards.**
16   ...
17   **You think I wanna go back to the bottom and start**
18   **cold-calling again? Fuck that. No way.** *(Beat)* **You know**
19   **what really gets me? I used to be with those people —**
20   **civil rights, affirmative action. Who knew?**
21   ...
22   **Of course they did. They were just waiting for a**
23   **cover like this Algaetech thing to pull the trigger.**
24   ...
25   **Biotech firm went bankrupt today — don't ask.**
26   **Listen to me, Eric. You're young; you've probably got**
27   **a head full of help-thy-neighbor idealism. Get rid of it.**
28   **Because when you get to be my age, you're gonna**
29   **have to drop your principles one by one, and it hurts,**
30   **kid. It hurts. Until this morning I was a liberal.**

1 ...
2   In my despair tonight, Eric, in the basement of
3 my pain, I got a sudden urge to come down here to
4 Strawberry Fields. And, funny thing, I started
5 thinking of the lyrics to "Imagine." You know,
6 "Imagine all the people ..." et cetera. John Lennon
7 was about my age when he got blown away. Saved
8 him, really. I mean, look what happened to George
9 and Ringo. And Paul. Turned into a vegetarian —
10 let Linda play on his albums. And I got to thinking
11 of my youth and how fucked up everything's gotten
12 since John was killed. I was in law school when it
13 happened — I was gonna do public interest, you
14 know? But it seemed like the whole optimism thing
15 went down with John. So I dropped out and got a
16 job on Wall Street. Until today. I never looked back.
17 *(Pause)* Anyway, right when I'm about to start
18 looking for my own personal Mark David Chapman,
19 I run into this black guy — don't ask me how — and
20 he says to me, totally out of the blue, he says,
21 "Have you been there for your son?" That just hit
22 me, Eric. Like on TV when they have that thing,
23 "Have you hugged your kid today?" and I think to
24 myself I haven't even seen my kid in months. I knew
25 right then I had to call you. *(Beat)* I don't think we
26 talk enough, Eric.
27
28
29
30
31
32
33
34
35

Shylock

by Mark Leiren-Young

1 Political correctness and the plays of William Shakespeare
2 come together in this monolog by Canadian Mark Leiren-Young's
3 *Shylock*. Jon Davies is an actor in his forties who is concerned with
4 the preservation of all of Shakespeare's works, whether they are
5 politically correct or not.
6
7
8 JON DAVIES: I fell in love with Shakespeare for the
9   stories. Not the words. When I visited my
10   grandmother at the home, when I was a kid, I always
11   used to stare at her bookshelf, which was mostly
12   cluttered up with pictures of family, photo albums,
13   and three books: the Torah, that's the old testament
14   — a prayer book and Shakespeare. It had well-worn
15   red leather bindings and the spine had an etching of
16   a man's face, Shakespeare's face, although I didn't
17   know that at the time. I thought it was a picture of a
18   sorcerer, perhaps even Merlin. And I thought the book
19   was a collection of magic spells. My grandmother was
20   so old that for all I knew she used to be friends with
21   Merlin. So on my thirteenth birthday my grandmother
22   gave me her copy of *The Collected Works* and I was
23   delighted. Until I went into my bedroom with my new
24   treasure, opened it up and discovered it was just a
25   bunch of stupid, boring plays written in very strange
26   English. There weren't even any pictures. I was
27   heartbroken. The closest I got to "literature" was
28   Batman. So I put the book on my shelf and I probably
29   would have forgotten all about it if not for a severe
30   case of the measles about a year later. It took me two

1   days to reread all my comic books. On day three I
2   started *King Lear.* I didn't understand all the
3   words, I didn't understand most of the words, but
4   somehow I managed to understand the story
5   because at about midnight on day four — as Lear
6   cradled his poor, lifeless Cordelia in his arms — I
7   began to cry. And it was the first time a story in a
8   book ever made me cry. There were no spells —
9   unless you count the incantations from the Scottish
10   play — but it was magic all the same. Unlike
11   Loffleur. I fell in love with Shakespeare for the
12   stories. But the words came a close second. They
13   may not taste like champagne or chocolate — not
14   to me anyway — but there's something very ...
15   fulfilling ... about speaking them. They make me
16   feel like the dream-speaker of the tribe, like I'm
17   seeing something that may be or ought to be or
18   simply was and shouldn't be forgotten. Fulfilling.
19   More fulfilling than that allergy commercial I did a
20   few months ago. You know the one. Except the
21   allergy commercial paid more than a full season at
22   the festival. So when the Festival approached me
23   about playing Shylock, Tony and I talked about the
24   play and agreed — this would be an attempt to do
25   Shylock the way he was written. So instead of
26   starting with Jew — I started with villain. Instead of
27   starting with outcast, I started with greed. And
28   vengeance. And the type of villain Shakespeare's
29   audience would have hated and booed and hissed.
30   Much the same way some people in the audience
31   for this show have hated and booed and hissed. The
32   type of villain Shakespeare actually wrote. Yes. A
33   negative character. So I started my research. I
34   looked at the great Shylocks in history. At Macklin
35   and Kean and the others who had played him

through the ages. And all the greats had started with the same impulse — either a clown, who the world would laugh at, or a tragic and sympathetic old man. A man worn down by the wrongs of society. A man the audience could pity and perhaps even love because, Christmas pantomimes aside, all actors want to be loved. But almost all these men ultimately changed their approach. The longer they played the role the more apparent it became that Shylock isn't a wronged hero or a pathetic old man — he's supposed to be the villain. And maybe there are moments the audience is supposed to feel for him, but no more than they're supposed to briefly feel for Richard the Third. If Shakespeare truly meant to create a story about a sympathetic Jew, if he truly wanted to create a plea for tolerance, surely he wouldn't have told the story of a cruel Jewish moneylender who lives for vengeance. Moneylender — a profession lower on the social ladder in his day than prostitute. Or actor. Any man who could create moments of sympathy for Richard the Third could surely have come up with a more appealing and honorable Jew than Shylock the moneylender. Shylock the fiend. If he wanted us to accept the Jew as human, why praise Jessica for her "Christian temperament." Why abuse and humiliate Shylock and demand that he convert?

Master of the Obvious

by Kevin Fisher

1   The father in Kevin Fisher's *Master of the Obvious* recalls his
2 daughter's birth, revealing his own struggle to cope with his wife's
3 compromised labor.
4

5

6 FATHER: My pregnant wife calls. They have her at the
7   hospital and they won't let her leave ... For the first
8   and only time in my life, I take a cab five blocks. They
9   have her on a monitor that spikes when the
10   contractions are coming so I can lean over my
11   sweating wife and tell her "It's coming" and she can
12   say "*I know.*" Parents are about the worst people
13   you'd ever want to meet. They all say, "Well, it'll
14   change your life" and I always say "No it won't," and
15   they say "Yes it will" and I say "No it won't," until
16   they give up and I'm left to talk to the single people.
17   Single people without pets. We'd gone to Bradley.
18   Which is Lamaze without ridiculous hyperventilating.
19   Bradley presents a view of natural childbirth that we
20   later realized was pure fantasy. Mothers through back
21   massage and creative visualizations — "de sand is
22   warm, the Caribbean water laps at your feet, you are
23   on vacation" — are supposed to be able to give birth
24   without any pain medication whatsoever. Dr. Bradley
25   says that mothers who take pain killers during birth
26   are giving their babies cocaine. I'd like to hear his
27   thoughts on prostate surgery. A friend of mine from
28   college inherited his family farm. The one time I
29   visited we went out looking for a lost pregnant cow. It
30   was almost dark when I found her in a pouring cold

1   rain. She was lying on her side, covered in mud,
2   breathing hard, drooling white foam. The calf's
3   head was sticking out dead. My friend went to get
4   the vet, and told me I had to get the cow up on her
5   feet or she'd die. So he gave me the cattle prod,
6   and for the next hour and a half I try to coax the
7   cow to get up with words, and eventually the
8   electric cattle prod. The vet comes and we pull out
9   the dead calf and ten feet of placenta. And my
10   friend shoots the cow because she's paralyzed. But
11   he doesn't tell me he's going to do this, he just says
12   "stand back" and I hear this *bang* and I get hit with
13   blood. This was my only prior birth experience.
14   After twelve hours at the hospital, my wife's only
15   contracted a bit, they want to put her on the "pit."
16   The "pit" is a drip IV of a drug that accelerates
17   contractions. For the next five hours my wife stands
18   bent over. She doesn't talk and she looks like she's
19   nine years old and she's experiencing over and over
20   watching her favorite dog being hit by a car again
21   every twenty seconds. We do not speak except
22   when she starts to get these fierce shakes on top of
23   the contractions, and I hear her whisper "Pet me
24   like a cat." And climbing over the tubes and
25   monitor and the nurses, I do. I've never seen
26   anyone really experience pain like this. After five
27   hours, my wife says "Give me the epidural." They
28   tap into her spine and for the first time in hours we
29   talk. They check her and she's over half dilated,
30   and so they want to break her water to push things
31   along. And they use what looks like a knitting
32   needle, and I ask her how it feels and she says "like
33   having someone scrape your bones with a cheese
34   grater." We have two good hours, but the fetal
35   heartbeat is really high. No one tells us this but we

1 can read the monitor and it's at 180 beats a
2 minute. And the Doctor comes in to say we have to
3 go off the pit to slow the heartbeat. And they take
4 her off the pit, and everyone leaves. And I
5 remember someone telling us that you know you're
6 in trouble if they start disappearing, because no
7 one wants to be in the room when something goes
8 wrong. Then the heartbeat goes to 209 a minute.
9 A few days later after we were home, I found a
10 metronome and I set it at 209. It's *prestissimo*. As
11 fast as music will go. Right now, my wife and I look
12 at each other and both know we can't go there.
13 Everyone has a dead baby or a umbilical cord story
14 they have to tell you. My response, if someone
15 starts to tell me about some umbilical cord that
16 acts like a malevolent garden hose, I say "That's
17 OK ... we're having one of the new cordless
18 babies." Someone tells us that more
19 hermaphrodite babies are being born. And in the
20 old days the doctor would flip a coin and decide the
21 sex, but now you have to wait till they're old
22 enough to make an informed choice. Assuming
23 they don't want the flexibility. Until then names are
24 a problem. My wife says she wants a C-section
25 now. They take her away to the O.R. I suit up in a
26 green paper suit, but before they let me in to see
27 my wife who's in the O.R., the nurses tell me I have
28 to check out of our room. I throw my wife's clothes
29 into the hallway and run to the O.R. In the
30 operating room, I crouch next to my wife as she lies
31 on the operating table. A curtain separates her
32 head and where the doctors work. And we pretend
33 she's not being operated on, but instead she's
34 merely trapped under a crane or a train or a
35 building and we're waiting for the rescue team.

1   After a while the doctor tells me to look and I look
2   and a purplish head and body comes out of a hole
3   in my wife's stomach ... like a roll of cookie dough
4   with eyes. I wait to leave until my wife is off her
5   oxygen mask. They want me to leave earlier, but I
6   keep coming back and they give up. Some young
7   guy who arrives with flowers after visiting hours
8   and wants to see one of the mothers on the floor.
9   And they won't let him in even though he tells them
10   he's the father. And the way he says it it's like the
11   first time he said it and it's a big deal confession,
12   and they still won't let him in and he leaves and I
13   wonder if he's ever coming back. At three in the
14   morning, I go by the nursery on my way home and
15   it's empty, except for a mid-aged nurse holding up
16   a loud screaming baby by one leg as she washes it
17   and I realize that's my daughter. And I feel scared.
18   And maybe I should go in and take her from the
19   nurse and wash her myself, but I don't because she
20   looks like a small animal, a small feral scary
21   animal. Having kids was sort of a leap of faith.
22   Parents keep saying you're going to love them
23   because they're so helpless. Because they need
24   you. I never got this because I don't like needy
25   people. Somehow I didn't experience that moment
26   I was supposed to have in the operating room —
27   which everyone says happens — when you look into
28   your daughter's eyes and you get it. You suddenly
29   understand your place in the universe. I realize I'm
30   not ready, and so I go home, and it's quiet there for
31   what I later realized was the last time, and I pour
32   myself a stiff drink and read Dr. Spock, but unlike
33   the other Spock this one has little to say about my
34   place in the universe.
35

Scenes for One Female and One Male

Arcadia

by Tom Stoppard

1   The innovative *Rosencrantz and Guildenstern Are Dead*
2 brought Tom Stoppard instant worldwide fame when it was first
3 performed in 1966. Since that time, British dramatist Stoppard's
4 reputation has continued to grow and he has received international
5 acclaim as one of the twentieth-century's greatest playwrights.
6 *Arcadia*, which premiered in 1993, is his best work and one of the
7 finest plays in theatre history. Set in two time periods, the drama
8 provides a perspective on the nature of human invention.
9
10
11 **THOMASINA: Oh, Septimus!–can you bear it? All the lost**
12   **plays of the Athenians! Two hundred at least by**
13   **Aeschylus, Sophocles, Euripides — thousands of**
14   **poems — Aristotle's own library brought to Egypt by**
15   **the noodle's ancestors! How can we sleep for grief?**
16 **SEPTIMUS: By counting our stock. Seven plays from**
17   **Aeschylus, seven from Sophocles, *nineteen* from**
18   **Euripides, my lady! You should no more grieve for the**
19   **rest than for a buckle lost from your first shoe, or for**
20   **your lesson book which will be lost when you are old.**
21   **We shed as we pick up, like travelers who must carry**
22   **everything in their arms, and what we let fall will be**
23   **picked up by those behind. The procession is very**
24   **long and life is very short. We die on the march. But**
25   **there is nothing outside the march so nothing can be**
26   **lost to it. The missing plays of Sophocles will turn up**
27   **piece by piece, or be written again in another**
28   **language. Ancient cures for diseases will reveal**
29   **themselves once more. Mathematical discoveries**
30   **glimpsed and lost to view will have their time again.**

1   **You do not suppose, my lady, that if all of**
2   **Archimedes had been hiding in the great library of**
3   **Alexandria, we would be at a loss for a corkscrew?**
4
5
6
7
8
9
10
11
12
13
14
15
16
17
18
19
20
21
22
23
24
25
26
27
28
29
30
31
32
33
34
35

Trudy Blue

by Marsha Norman

1   Marsha Norman's most widely produced drama is *Night*
2 *Mother*, the winner of the 1983 Pulitzer Prize for drama. Her
3 second most famous work, *Trudy Blue*, was first mounted in 1994.
4 The following scene serves as a prologue for the play.
5
6
7 **GINGER: How's your mother feeling? Did you talk to her**
8   **today?** *(DON doesn't answer. She closes her book.)* **I'm**
9   **going downstairs. Do you want anything?** *(She sits up.)*
10   **Like a glass of water or anything?** *(She looks over at*
11   *him.)* **Don?**
12 **DON: I said "no."**
13 **GINGER: You did?**
14 **DON: There's something the matter with your hearing,**
15   **have you noticed? Especially on the phone.** *(Imitating*
16   *her.)* **What? What?**
17 **GINGER: My hearing?**
18 **DON: Your hearing. Don't stay up too late. How late were**
19   **you up last night?**
20 **GINGER: I don't know. Three.**
21 **DON: Oh. If you'll give me the registration for the Volvo,**
22   **I'll take it out with me tomorrow and put it on.**
23 **GINGER: You're going to the country tomorrow?**
24 **DON: I told you that. Jesus, Ginger. Just for the day,**
25   **though. I'll be back by eight.**
26 **GINGER: You told me you were going to the country? What**
27   **is tomorrow?**
28 **DON: Tuesday. Yes. I told you. I rented a workshop.**
29 **GINGER: A workshop?**
30 **DON: Yes. If you will remember our discussion last**

1 weekend, I can either stop making tables
2 altogether, or just stop making them in the house.
3 So I rented a workshop.
4 GINGER: It wasn't about the tables. It was about the
5 time you spend making the tables. It was about how
6 I don't see you. About how the first thing you do
7 when we get out to the house is leave.
8 DON: I'm not leaving. Ginger. I'm getting the mail.
9 GINGER: Checking on the boat. Going to the hardware
10 store. The liquor store. The bait store. Buying
11 magazines. Getting the cars washed, the oil
12 changed, the tanks filled, the mats cleaned. Buying
13 trash bags. Lightbulbs. Tape. Dog food. Bird food.
14 Fish food.
15 DON: Do you think I like doing those things?
16 GINGER: I don't know, Don.
17 DON: If you didn't want any animals, you should've told
18 the kids no.
19 GINGER: That would have been popular.
20 DON: Since when did you worry about being popular?
21 GINGER: What are you going to do in your shop?
22 DON: Make tables.
23 GINGER: To sell?
24 DON: No, not to sell. It would be really stupid to take
25 the one thing I really enjoy doing, and turn it into
26 work.
27 GINGER: But your tables are beautiful. People love them.
28 You should take one out to Ralph Lauren and —
29 DON: Just stop it, Ginger. OK? I'm never going to make
30 any more money than I do right now. And I'm never
31 going to like what I do. And if that means I'm never
32 going to be good enough for you, then that's just
33 too bad. This is who I am. And this is who you
34 married.
35 GINGER: I'm sorry. It's just I keep thinking —

1   **DON: Stop thinking. Stop thinking about what would**
2   **make my life more interesting to you. I am not a**
3   **character in your new novel. I'm your husband. Cut**
4   **me some slack.** *(She gets out of the bed, puts on her*
5   *slippers and robe. DON looks up.)*
6   **DON: Would you bring me a glass of water when you**
7   **come up?**
8   **GINGER: I could be a while. Do you want me to bring it**
9   **up right now?**
10   **DON: That would be great. Thanks.**
11   **GINGER: You're going to move all your equipment into**
12   **this shop?**
13   **DON: I have to have a place to go, Ginger. What do you**
14   **want me to do, hang around the house all weekend**
15   **and watch you read?**
16   **GINGER: Do you want ice in your water?**
17   **DON: That would be great. Thanks. I love you.**
18   **GINGER: I love you too. Goodnight.** *(She goes out the*
19   *door.)*
20
21
22
23
24
25
26
27
28
29
30
31
32
33
34
35

Nightmare
by Steven H. Gale

1　Steven Gale's *Nightmare* is based on an actual incident. It is
2　included here in its entirety.

3　**DRAMATIS PERSONAE:**
4

5　**HUSBAND** — an ordinary, middle-class professional man, still
6　　youngish, but moving into middle age. He is tired, defeated.

7
8　**WIFE** — an ordinary, middle-class housewife, possibly a few years
9　　younger than her husband. She, too, is tired, defeated.

10　**SCENE:** *As the curtain rises we discover HUSBAND, shirt*
11　　*sleeves rolled up, tie loose, and WIFE sitting across from*
12　　*one another at a small kitchen table in the center of the*
13　　*stage. There is a telephone on the wall.*
14　　　*It is night. Lights are up on the couple; the rest of the set*
15　　*is dim.*
16　　　*The setting is simple, meant more to suggest than to state*
17　　*— it is a middle-class kitchen, pleasant, not overly fancy.*
18　　*Only the outlines of the room are indicated, by two-by-fours,*
19　　*curtains, etc., with a few modern electrical appliances*
20　　*scattered around to let us know what room it is and the taste*
21　　*and class level of the two people sitting in it.*
22　　　*For several moments the couple sits in silence, heads*
23　　*partly bowed, not really looking at each other. When they*
24　　*speak, it is in low tones.*
25　**HUSBAND: What are we going to do?** *(Pause)*
26　**WIFE: I don't know.**
27　**HUSBAND: But we have to do something ...**
28　**WIFE: What? What can we do?**
29　**HUSBAND: Didn't they tell you what to do? Didn't they say**
30　　**if they're going to do anything?**

1   **WIFE:** They told me to keep her home. *(Pause)*

2   **HUSBAND:** How long?

3   **WIFE:** What?

4   **HUSBAND:** How long did they tell you to keep her home?

5   **WIFE:** *(Thinking)* I don't know. **Forever.** *(Pause. HUSBAND*

6   *stands, paces a few steps, turns to WIFE.)*

7   **HUSBAND:** Let's go over it again.

8   **WIFE:** Why?

9   **HUSBAND:** Maybe we can figure out what's happening,

10   who it is, why he's doing it.

11   **WIFE:** We've tried.

12   **HUSBAND:** Try again.

13   **WIFE:** *(Sighs.)* I was in the living room, cleaning ...

14   **HUSBAND:** *(Interrupting)* No, no. What did the principal

15   say when he called?

16   **WIFE:** He said somebody called and asked for Linda.

17   **HUSBAND:** Who?

18   **WIFE:** Some man.

19   **HUSBAND:** And?

20   **WIFE:** And this guy said he was a doctor and that I was

21   hurt and could he pick Linda up and take her to the

22   hospital to see me because I was worried and

23   asking about her. *(Pause. HUSBAND walks back and*

24   *sits down again. WIFE gets up and walks slowly to the*

25   *cabinet at the back of the kitchen and stands there*

26   *facing the wall.)*

27   **HUSBAND:** What happened then?

28   **WIFE:** *(Slightly hysterical)* He told him that they couldn't

29   release children to anyone but their parents, and

30   the man hung up.

31   **HUSBAND:** *(Banging his fist on the table)* **Jesus!** *(Short*

32   *pause)* Why in the hell didn't he tell him to come and

33   pick her up, then call you to find out if you were

34   alright and call the police? He could have had them

35   waiting for him!

1   WIFE: *(Walking back to the table)* I don't know. He didn't
2   think about it I guess.
3   HUSBAND: *(Exasperatedly)* Jesus. *(WIFE sits down. Pause.)*
4   Did he say what the guy said his name was or what
5   hospital it was supposed to be?
6   WIFE: I don't think so ... I don't think he remembered.
7   HUSBAND: And we're trusting our daughter's education
8   to this guy? *(Pause)* You don't know the name then?
9   WIFE: No ... Does it matter?
10 HUSBAND: No. Probably not. *(Pause)*
11 WIFE: What are we going to do?
12 HUSBAND: I don't know ... I don't know. *(Pause)* Christ,
13   can't they give us any help?
14 WIFE: He said that once she was off the school grounds
15   she was our responsibility.
16 HUSBAND: And we're not supposed to send her back to
17   school.
18 WIFE: No.
19 HUSBAND: Why not?
20 WIFE: He said they can't take the responsibility. There's
21   really no way to protect her there or on the way
22   home.
23 HUSBAND: *(Shouting)* But that's their job! They're
24   supposed to take care of her when she's in school!
25 WIFE: *(Hissing)* Quiet! You'll wake her up. *(Silence)* Did
26   you hear something?
27 HUSBAND: No.
28 WIFE: I thought I heard her. I'm going to take a look.
29   *(The WIFE gets up and walks out of the room. The
30   HUSBAND sits motionless, waiting for her to come
31   back. She returns after a short time.)*
32 WIFE: It wasn't anything. She's still asleep.
33 HUSBAND: Let me get this clear. She's got to stay here
34   in the house ... for how long?
35 WIFE: For the rest of the year. Who knows?

1   HUSBAND: We're supposed to take her out of school
2   completely.
3   WIFE: That's right. He did say that maybe she could go
4   to some other school next year.
5   HUSBAND: Where?
6   WIFE: He didn't know. He thought maybe it might be
7   best to send her to some other district.
8   HUSBAND: But why?
9   WIFE: Because he knows her. He knows who she is.
10   *(Short pause)* He knows her name and what she
11   looks like and where she lives. *(Pause)*
12   HUSBAND: They don't have any way of finding out who
13   it was?
14   WIFE: No.
15   HUSBAND: Linda doesn't know him?
16   WIFE: No ...
17   HUSBAND: But he knows her name and where she goes
18   to school! How'd he find out? Where'd he meet
19   her? How does he know who she is?
20   WIFE: You know how friendly she is, always talking to
21   everyone.
22   HUSBAND: *(Begging, plaintively)* But we've told her *not*
23   *to talk to strangers.*
24   WIFE: I know, and she doesn't really, but if she was at
25   the bus stop on the way to school and someone
26   started talking to her, she'd tell him her name. And
27   he could figure out where she went to school. Or
28   maybe he followed her there. Or here. *(Pause)*
29   HUSBAND: We don't really even know why he wanted
30   her, do we?
31   WIFE: No. *(Silence. The telephone rings, loudly, jarringly.*
32   *HUSBAND and WIFE are startled. They look at the*
33   *phone and then stare at each other. The phone*
34   *continues to ring. Finally, WIFE gets up slowly and*
35   *answers the phone.)*

1   **WIFE:** *(In an apprehensive tone)* **Hello? ... Yes ... Yes, he's**
2   **here too ... No, no, she's asleep ... Yes, I think**
3   **she's all right. She doesn't seem to understand**
4   **what's happening ... No ... Thank you ... OK ...**
5   **Why? ... But I don't understand! ... But what if I ...**
6   **But, but, why? ... And that's the only way —** *(Her*
7   *voice is now flat, emotionless.)* **... All right, I'll tell him**
8   **... Yes. Goodnight.** *(WIFE sits back down and sobs*
9   *quietly. HUSBAND watches her, dumbfounded,*
10   *frustrated. He reaches over and grabs her arm.)*
11   **HUSBAND: What is it? Who was it?**
12   **WIFE: It was the principal.**
13   **HUSBAND: What'd that ass want?**
14   **WIFE: He wanted to make it clear that he thinks we**
15   **ought to move away from here. Clear out of the**
16   **state, if possible.**
17   **HUSBAND: What! He said that? Why?**
18   **WIFE: Because the guy knows where she lives and she'll**
19   **never be safe. He could come along anytime or just**
20   **wait until we send her to another school and follow**
21   **her again.**
22   **HUSBAND: Couldn't you take her to school?**
23   **WIFE: Yes, but I still couldn't watch her all the time, and**
24   **he might try to get her at school again, out on the**
25   **playground or something.**
26   **HUSBAND: But move clear out of the state?**
27   **WIFE: That's what he said.**
28   **HUSBAND: What about my work? I can't just get up and**
29   **move out of here. What about my job?**
30   **WIFE: He said he was sorry, but that's the only way she**
31   **could really be safe.** *(Long pause)* **He said something**
32   **else, too ... He said that if this guy really wants to**
33   **get her, he might follow us even if we leave the**
34   **state. There's no way we can know. There's no way**
35   **we can ever know if she'll be safe again. He could**

1   **show up anywhere ... Any time.** *(Silence)* **What are**
2   **we going to do?** *(Silence)*
3
4 *Curtain*
5
6
7
8
9
10
11
12
13
14
15
16
17
18
19
20
21
22
23
24
25
26
27
28
29
30
31
32
33
34
35

Unanswered Invocation
A Play in Ten Minutes
by Shannon Gale

1   Shannon Gale's *Unanswered Invocation*, her second
2 performed drama, was featured at the Delaware Ten-Minute Play
3 Festival in 1998. About the interpersonal relationship between a
4 young woman and a young man, it is included here in its entirety.
5
6
7   **RACHEL:** *(Out of the darkness)*
8   **Oh! Richard, my muse, my almost-muse,**
9   **my ghost, sing to me, you silent spectral**
10   **of night and dreams, of breath and bright, of hope.**
11   **Sing, sing to me, you! Forget the softness**
12   **dancing on your skin and take upon**
13   **your shapeless shape the cloak of villainy —**
14   **my villain and my tempter! Conjure songs**
15   **from graves unmarked or coldly etched with Bach,**
16   **Beethoven, Brahms, and Liszt, or those still**
17   **upon the carver's block just marked with "Rich."**
18   **Steal, if you must, offend and rape the arts,**
19   **but Oh! my God, my God! Take shape, take form,**
20   **take voice! And speak and sing and laugh out loud.**
21   **My God, my muse, my ghost. Speak! Sing!**
22   **Take me again into your bonds, your haunting**
23   **chains, and stir my inspiration. Sing!**
24 **RICHARD:** *(Assuming character)* **I once knew a man who**
25   **could pull a rabbit from a hat. He wore a whisker**
26   **beneath his nose, a shine on the tip of his boot, and**
27   **an exact air not of being somewhere where he did not**
28   **belong, but of being somewhere which did not belong**
29   **to him.**
30 **RACHEL: Tell me, is it but a dream when I remember**

1 things we've never done?
2 RICHARD: *(As if giving dictation)* **I once knew a man who**
3   **could pull a rabbit from a hat ...**
4 RACHEL: When I remember things we've never done, is
5   it just a dream or is it love?
6 RICHARD: He stood affectedly over the gravel, and when
7   I passed, asked if I should like to see a man pull a
8   rabbit from a hat. He said so should he, if the man
9   would presume to attempt the trick without knowing
10   the near whereabouts of a rabbit beforehand.
11 RACHEL: I see no rabbit.
12 RICHARD: *(In a tone of conversation)* **I see no hat.**
13 RACHEL: You spoke as if you knew my name.
14 RICHARD: Rachel.
15 RACHEL: *(Into the darkness)*
16   Oh sing of valleys, meadows, streams, laughing
17   pebbled brooks and wildest flowers swaying
18   upon the gentle impulses of dreams
19   and sighs who dance upon the glittered wings
20   of butterflies. And sing of happiness
21   and free blue skies, and tell the secret joy
22   of looking through the soft transparency
23   of shadows. Hum the closed-eye mirth of Earth
24   in all her glory and life and all in love.
25 RICHARD: *(Assuming character)* **I saw your eyes glitter in**
26   **recognition when your sister called. Rachel. I knew**
27   **your name, but it did not matter.**
28 RACHEL: It did matter.
29 RICHARD: It did not matter. I knew your eyes, the glitter
30   of ...
31 RACHEL: It did matter in the crowd of the country fair.
32   The heavy scent of greasy food and cotton candy —
33   you spoke as if you knew my name.
34 RICHARD: *(Giving dictation)* **He stood affectedly over the**
35   **fairground gravel and smiled at the air as if it was**

1   a passerby. "Should you like to see a man pull a
2   rabbit from a hat?"
3 RACHEL: You never pulled a rabbit from a hat.
4 RICHARD: Once I met a man who could pull ...
5 RACHEL: You never did. Was that a lie?
6 RICHARD: Rachel. He spoke as if he knew my name.
7 RACHEL: When writing from the heart, can any thing
8   appear except the truth or what the truth
9   might have been if all that passed before
10   had been a dream? Does any soul care
11   which truth is told if truth is told at all?
12 RICHARD: All the past is truth, and all truth is in the
13   past.
14 RACHEL: The future. *(Richard picks up a hat.)* **You are**
15   **making jokes as I lie dying.** *(Richard taps the hat with*
16   *a magician's touch.)* **Curse you for toying with the**
17   **truth with a dying woman, weak and diseased.**
18 RICHARD: *(Assuming character)* **I did not know.**
19 RACHEL: You'll come to see me? In the end, when I am
20   on the bed. You'll come?
21 RICHARD: You are dying?
22 RACHEL: And if not?
23 RICHARD: Dying?
24 RACHEL: Every day. Some are good and some are bad.
25   It is slow.
26 RICHARD: I will be here.
27 RACHEL: It is hard, this dying, when life is so beautiful,
28   there is so much.
29 RICHARD: You are beautiful.
30 RACHEL: *(Continuing)* **Blessed beyond my desserts.**
31   **Except, of course, for the disease. A little more every**
32   **day, diseased. Until deceased.** *(Pause)* **But there are**
33   **good days, when I forget you're gone or when I am**
34   **filled with everything else. But the bad days come**
35   **unexpectedly. Sometimes it is the weather.**

1   Sometimes it is, I do not know. Sometimes.

2   RICHARD: Dying?

3   RACHEL: More than you.

4   RICHARD: Until you — and then I immediately without

5   a choice.

6   RACHEL: But I might die for decades before the end

7   while you live for decades before you die.

8   RICHARD: Your life is mine and so your death.

9   RACHEL: It is a trick.

10   RICHARD: *(In a tone of conversation)* I'm only playing

11   along.

12   RACHEL: Stop. *(Pause)* Sing.

13   RICHARD: You know I can't.

14   RACHEL: Play upon some instrument. *(Pause)* Impostor!

15   You are no musician.

16   RICHARD: I am a disease.

17   RACHEL: You are nothing.

18   RICHARD: I have effect. The truth does not matter and

19   Richard is nothing and less because I am what you

20   believe. *(He magically takes a bottle of pills from the*

21   *hat.)* I could make you swallow a pill.

22   RACHEL: What are those?

23   RICHARD: I have been suicidal before.

24   RACHEL: What?

25   RICHARD: I left you for Jessica, and she left me.

26   RACHEL: That is of no concern to me.

27   RICHARD: You cursed her name.

28   RACHEL: No, I detested it. What is it: Jessica. How can

29   you love "Jessica"? If it were Suzanne or Bethany

30   or Julia. A powerful name or sweet, a name of a

31   woman you could respect, admire, then I could

32   understand.

33   RICHARD: A rose by another name.

34   RACHEL: Shut up. *(Pause. RICHARD drops the rattling pill*

35   *bottle back into the hat, then turns the hat over. The*

1   *pills cease to rattle and do not fall out.)* **You put them**
2   **away?**
3   RICHARD: You wouldn't do it.
4   RACHEL: I am too strong.
5   RICHARD: No, that is not it. You wouldn't do it because
6   there is still hope, or rather, because you still hope
7   when there is no more.
8   RACHEL: I see her in every woman's face.
9   RICHARD: Jessica could be anyone. You have never
10   met. But she has seen your photos, and she
11   watches you, perhaps, as a woman in a bookstore
12   or in a car or at a cafe spies a shopper who was her
13   lover's last. And she sees in you what failed.
14   RACHEL: It is not failure.
15   RICHARD: *(Assuming character)* **In a house of mazes, we**
16   **kissed in the dark. My back against the trailer wall**
17   **and his warm hands large and sure.**
18   RACHEL: It was not like that.
19   RICHARD: **And a clown laughed outside at distorted**
20   **images in crooked mirrors.**
21   RACHEL: You're forgetting the romance.
22   RICHARD: **In the dark, though I could not see him, he**
23   **had an exact air not of being somewhere where he**
24   **belonged, but of being somewhere that belonged to**
25   **him. His hands were large and strong.**
26   RACHEL: Don't you know a song?
27   RICHARD: *(Singing)* **Row, row, row your boat**
28   **gently down the stream,**
29   **merrily, merrily, merrily, merrily.**
30   **Life is but a dream.**
31   RACHEL: *(After song is started)* **He had a voice that could**
32   **melt an angel's knees, and he studied the songs of**
33   **birds calling to each other in the trees and learned**
34   **their varied melodies.** *(When Richard's song is*
35   *finished)* **Very funny.**

1   RICHARD: There is the song I sang as I left you.

2   RACHEL: How does it go?

3   RICHARD: *(Singing)* You fill up my senses like a night in

4   the forest, like a ...

5   RACHEL: It hurts so much. *(Pause)* It hurts so much! To

6   watch you moving about in his shape, in this

7   holographic image of who he was, and speaking in

8   my words. Speaking back to me in my own words

9   and not a bit of flesh to touch for comfort. Can't he

10   know from his distance that I have made myself

11   beautiful and strong and ambitious for him, for him

12   to find me worthy of his life. Can't he see my body's

13   form, the colors in my face, and be pulled to it from

14   his distance. I did not ask you, ghost, to come here

15   into my thoughts to intrude villainously upon my

16   stale loneliness ... and if I did, it is only out of habit

17   of being unanswered, out of habit of disappointment

18   and expectation. Release me!

19   RICHARD: I released you long ago.

20   RACHEL: Speak up. You use my own words. Say them

21   so that I can hear.

22   RICHARD: *(Speaking and then melting quickly into song)* I

23   released ... you fill up my senses like a night in the

24   forest, like a ...

25   RACHEL: His words, they sound so like his words.

26   *(Richard circles one hand over the hat.)*

27   RICHARD: He let you go.

28   RACHEL: What?

29   RICHARD: He let go of you. A long time ago. You are

30   free.

31   RACHEL: Then what are you doing here?

32   RICHARD: Let go.

33   RACHEL: I don't want to let go. I want to love him. I

34   want him to come back to me and let me love him

35   and love me. If I let you go, he will be lost forever.

1   RICHARD: There is more than one way to be lost. In a
2   maze, there are many dead ends, many false turns,
3   even crooked mirrors, but there is only one way out.
4   RACHEL: What if I don't want out?
5   RICHARD: You have to come out eventually. There is no
6   immortal lost.
7   RACHEL: Give me those pills.
8   RICHARD: That is not what I meant.
9   RACHEL: I want the pills. What are they?
10 RICHARD: That is not what he would want.
11 RACHEL: But that doesn't matter, right? *(Pause.*
12   *RICHARD pulls the pills again from the hat and hands*
13   *them to RACHEL.)*
14 RICHARD: They're just — I wasn't that serious before —
15   sleeping pills. You'll have to take them all.
16 RACHEL: It is better so. No romance in the end, with the
17   one poisonous kiss, but instead the hideous act of
18   swallowing a hundred hard, sickening little pills.
19 RICHARD: There is more than one way.
20 RACHEL: Crush them and put them in water.
21 RICHARD: Out of the maze. I was wrong. There are
22   many ways.
23 RACHEL: Then why should anyone ever get lost?
24 RICHARD: You get lost when you stop trying. And it
25   isn't lost, really, because you know what got you
26   there, and you know that all you have to do to get
27   out is to try, but you stare in the darkness at a
28   blank wall, and perhaps even enjoy the hardness of
29   it against your nose in the dark.
30 RACHEL: *(Indicating the pills)* **Take these.** *(RICHARD does*
31   *not take the pills but puts the hat on his head and*
32   *disappears.)*
33 RACHEL: My precious cat — he has a handsome set
34   of whiskers and thinks he is a king of course
35   stretches his skinny legs and claws at my door

1   when he is bored with sleep. (Between
2   the meals and chases he has nothing more
3   to do but nap and I wonder what he dreams.)
4   The simple fact of pushing open the door
5   eludes him in his carefree, happy, Cat
6   World where watching birds and chasing bugs
7   playfully about is not as fun
8   as scratching at the door without a hope
9   of getting out (it's never worked before).
10
11
12
13
14
15
16
17
18
19
20
21
22
23
24
25
26
27
28
29
30
31
32
33
34
35

In Shakespeare and the Bible
by Thornton Wilder

1 Thornton Wilder is best-known for the popular award-winning
2 *Our Town*. Although Wilder died in 1975, some of his work has
3 never been produced and some has been produced only recently. *In*
4 *Shakespeare and the Bible* premiered at the Actors Theatre of
5 Louisville in 1997. This selection is about a young man who is
6 interested in an older woman's young niece.
7
8
9 **MRS. MOWBREY: Mr. Lubbock, I am Mrs. Mowbrey.**
10 **LUBBOCK: Good afternoon, ma'am.**
11 **MRS. MOWBREY: You don't know who I am?**
12 **LUBBOCK: No, ma'am. I got your letter asking me to call.**
13 **MRS. MOWBREY:** *(Coming forward)* **Won't you sit down?**
14 *(They sit, Mrs. Mowbrey behind the taboret.)* **Mr. Lubbock,**
15 **I had two reasons for asking you to call today. In the**
16 **first place, I wish to engage a lawyer. I thought we**
17 **might take a look at one another and see if we could**
18 **work together.** *(She pauses. He bows his head slightly and*
19 *impersonally.)* **I mean a lawyer to handle my affairs in**
20 **general and to advise me.** *(Same business)* **My second**
21 **reason for asking to see you is that I am your fiancée's**
22 **aunt.**
23 **LUBBOCK:** *(Amazed)* **Miss Buckingham's aunt! She never**
24 **told me she had an aunt.**
25 **MRS. MOWBREY: No, Mr. Lubbock, she wouldn't. I am the**
26 **black sheep of the family. My name is not mentioned**
27 **in that house. Will you pour me some port, please? I**
28 **am glad to see that you have helped yourself ... Thank**
29 **you ... Yes, I am your future mother-in-law's sister.** *(He*
30 *is standing up, holding his glass — waiting.)* **Our lives**

1   took different directions. *(He sits down.)* **But before**
2   **we get into the legal matter, let's get to know one**
3   **another a little better. Tell me, I haven't seen my**
4   **niece for fifteen years. Is she a pretty girl?**
5   LUBBOCK: Yes — very.
6   MRS. MOWBREY: We're a good-looking family.
7   LUBBOCK: *(Indicating the pictures on the wall)* **And a**
8   **distinguished one. Miss Buckingham would be very**
9   **interested in seeing these family portraits.**
10 MRS. MOWBREY: Yes. *(She sips her wine, then says dryly,*
11   *without a smile.)* **It's not hard to find family portraits,**
12   **Mr. Lubbock. There are places on Twelfth Street,**
13   **simply full of them. Bishops and generals —**
14   **whatever you want.**
15 LUBBOCK: *(Continuing to look at them, also without a*
16   *smile)* **Very fine collection, I should say.** *(She takes*
17   *another sip of wine.)*
18 MRS. MOWBREY: Mr. Lubbock, I've made some inquiries
19   about you. You are twenty-seven years old.
20 LUBBOCK: Yes, I am.
21 MRS. MOWBREY: You took your time finding yourself,
22   didn't you? All that unpleasantness down in
23   Philadelphia. What happened exactly? Well, we
24   won't go into it. Then you gave yourself a good
25   shaking. You pulled yourself together. Law school
26   — very good. People are still wondering where you
27   got all that spending money. It wasn't horse racing.
28   It wasn't cards. No one could figure it out.
29   Apparently it was something you were doing up in
30   Harlem. Certainly, your parents couldn't afford to
31   give you anything. In fact, you were very generous
32   to them. You bought them a house on Staten
33   Island. You were a very good son to them and I
34   think you'll make a very good family man.
35 LUBBOCK: *(With a slight bow and a touch of dry irony)* **You**

1   are very well informed, ma'am.
2   MRS. MOWBREY: Yes, I am. *(She takes another sip of*
3   *wine.)* **On Saturday nights you often went to 321**
4   **West Street — "The Palace," you boys called it.**
5   **Nice girls, every one of them, especially Dolores.**
6   LUBBOCK: *(Mastering violence, rises.)* **I don't like this**
7   **conversation, ma'am. I shall ask you to let me take**
8   **my leave.**
9   MRS. MOWBREY: *(Raising her voice)* **You and I have met**
10   **before, Mr. Lubbock. You knew me under another**
11   **name. I owned The Palace.**
12   LUBBOCK: Mrs. Higgins!
13   MRS. MOWBREY: My hair is no longer blond. *(She rises*
14   *and crosses the room.)* **You may leave any moment**
15   **you wish, but I never believed you were a hypocrite.**
16   LUBBOCK: *(After returning her fixed gaze wrathfully; then*
17   *sitting down again)* **What do you want?**
18   MRS. MOWBREY: Yes, I owned The Palace and several
19   other establishments — refined, very refined in
20   every way. I've sold them. I've retired. I see no one
21   — no one — whom I knew in those days. Except
22   today I am seeing yourself. Naturally, I am never
23   going to mention these matters again. I am going to
24   forget them, and I hope that you will forget them,
25   too. But it would be very valuable to me to have a
26   lawyer who knew them and who was in a position
27   to forget them. — I'll have a little more port, if
28   you'll be so good. *(Lubbock takes the glass from her*
29   *hand in silence, fills it at the taboret and carries it to her.*
30   *She murmurs: "Thank you." He returns and stands by*
31   *the taboret, talking to her across the length of the stage.)*
32   LUBBOCK: I don't believe you asked me here to engage
33   me as your lawyer. There's something else on your
34   mind. Will you say it and then let me take my leave?
35   MRS. MOWBREY: You were always like that, Jack.

1   **LUBBOCK:** *(Loudly)* **I will ask you not to call me Jack.**
2   **MRS. MOWBREY:** *(Bowing her head slightly)* **That was**
3   **always your way, Mr. Lubbock. Suspicious. Quick**
4   **to fight. Imagining that everybody was trying to**
5   **take advantage of you.**
6   **LUBBOCK: What do you want? I don't know what**
7   **you're talking about.** *(He starts with fuming lowered*
8   *head for the door.)* **Good afternoon.**
9   **MRS. MOWBREY: Mr. Lubbock, I will tell you what I**
10   **want.** *(He pauses with his back to her.)* **I am a rich**
11   **woman and I intend to get richer. And I am a lonely**
12   **woman, and I don't think that that is necessary. I**
13   **want to live. And when you and Katy are married,**
14   **I want you to help me.** *(He is "caught" and half turns.)*
15   **I want company. I want to entertain. I also want to**
16   **help people. I want — so to speak — to adopt**
17   **some. Not *young* children, of course, but young**
18   **men and women who want bringing out in some**
19   **way or other. I have a gift for that kind of thing. —**
20   **Even in my former work I was able to do all sorts**
21   **of things for my girls. Did you ever hear anyone say**
22   **that Mrs. Higgins was mean — unkind — to the**
23   **girls in her place?** *(He refuses to answer; the port is*
24   *going to her head. She strikes her bosom emotionally.)*
25   **I'm kind to a fault. I love to see young people**
26   *happy.* **Dozens of those girls — I helped them get**
27   **married. I encouraged them to find good homes.**
28   **Against my own interest. Your friend, Dolores**
29   **married a policeman. Happy as a lark.** *(She puts a*
30   *delicate lace handkerchief to her eyes and then to her*
31   *nose.)* **Will you consent to be my lawyer?**
32   **LUBBOCK:** *(Scorn and finality)* **My firm doesn't allow us**
33   **to serve family connections.**
34   **MRS. MOWBREY: Oh, I don't want to have anything to**
35   **do with that wretched firm: Wilbraham, Clayton,**

1   what's-its-name? All you do for me will be on your
2   own time. I shall start giving you three thousand a
3   year for your advice. Then —
4   LUBBOCK: I beg your pardon. It's entirely out of the
5   question.
6   MRS. MOWBREY: *(After a slight pause; in a less emotional*
7   *voice)* Yes, yes. I know that you are always ready
8   with your no! no! You haven't yet heard what I can
9   do for you. And I don't mean in the sense of money.
10   There is something you are greatly in need of ...
11   *(Pause)* ... John Lubbock. One can see that you are
12   a lawyer — and a very good one, I suspect. So, you
13   looked about you and you selected my niece?
14   LUBBOCK: Oh, much more than that. I'm very much in
15   love with your niece. You should know her. Katy's
16   an extraordinary girl.
17   MRS. MOWBREY: Is she? There's nothing very extraordinary
18   about her mother. What's extraordinary about Katy?
19   LUBBOCK: Why, she's ... I feel that I'm the luckiest man
20   in the world.
21   MRS. MOWBREY: Come now, Mr. Lubbock. You don't
22   have to talk like that to me.
23   LUBBOCK: *(Earnestly)* I assure you, I mean it.
24   MRS. MOWBREY: *(A touch of contempt)* Very clever, is
25   she? Reads a lot of books and all that kind of thing?
26   LUBBOCK: No-o. *(With a slight laugh)* But she asks a lot
27   of questions.
28   MRS. MOWBREY: *(Pleased)* Does she? So do I, Mr.
29   Lubbock, as you have noticed. *(She rises and starts*
30   *toward her former seat by the decanter of port.)* She
31   asks lots of questions. I like that. — I asked her to
32   call this afternoon.
33   LUBBOCK: *(Startled and uneasy)* You did? Did you tell her
34   that I would be here?
35   MRS. MOWBREY: No. I thought I would surprise her.

1 LUBBOCK: Katy doesn't like surprises. *(Preparing to leave,*
2   *with hand outstretched)* **I think that at your first**
3   **meeting with — after so long a time — you should see**
4   **her alone. Perhaps I can call on you at another time.**
5 MRS. MOWBREY: *(Still standing)* **What are you so nervous**
6   **about? It's not time for her to come yet, and besides**
7   **I have this law matter to discuss with you.**
8 LUBBOCK: Thank you. — I'll ask if I can call some other
9   time.
10 MRS. MOWBREY: Anyway, perhaps she won't come.
11   She'll have shown my letter to her mother and her
12   mother will have forbidden her to come. Would
13   Katy disobey her mother?
14 LUBBOCK: Yes.
15 MRS. MOWBREY: *(Eyeing him)* **Has Katy chosen to**
16   **marry you against her mother's wishes?**
17 LUBBOCK: Yes. Very much so.
18 MRS. MOWBREY: I see. Tears? Scenes? Slamming of
19   doors?
20 LUBBOCK: Yes, I think so.
21 MRS. MOWBREY: *(Leaning toward him confidentially,*
22   *lifted finger)* **Katy is like me, Mr. Lubbock. I can feel**
23   **it with every word you say.** *(Still uneasy, Lubbock has*
24   *been taking a few steps around the room; he looks up at*
25   *the ceiling and weighs this thoughtfully.)*
26 LUBBOCK: If you told her you were her aunt ... Yes, I
27   think she will come. Katy likes to know ... where she
28   stands; what it's all about, and that kind of thing.
29 MRS. MOWBREY: I see. A lawyer's wife. As you
30   suggested a few moments ago: she's inquisitive?
31 LUBBOCK: *(With a nervous laugh)* **Yes, she is.**
32 MRS. MOWBREY: And you think I'm inquisitive, too —
33   don't you?
34 LUBBOCK: Yes, I do.
35 MRS. MOWBREY: Well, let me tell you something, Mr.

1   **Lubbock. Everybody says we women are inquisitive.**
2   **Most of us are. We have to be. I wouldn't give a**
3   **cent for a woman who wasn't. And why?** *(The wine*
4   *has gone to her head. She emphasizes what she is about*
5   *to say by tapping with jeweled rings on the taboret.)*
6   **Because a good deal is asked of us for which we are**
7   **not prepared. Women have to keep their wits about**
8   **them to survive at all, Mr. Lubbock.** *(She leans back*
9   *in her chair.)* **When I was married I didn't hesitate to**
10   **read every scrap of paper my husband left lying**
11   **around the house. But** *(She leans forward)* **as I said,**
12   **I have some business to discuss with you before**
13   **Katy comes. — Do you always walk about that way?**
14 **LUBBOCK:** *(Surprised)* **People tell me I do. I do in court.**
15   **If it makes you uneasy —**
16 **MRS. MOWBREY: I would like to ask another thing.**
17   **When you are married — and as a wedding present**
18   **I shall give Katy a very large check, I assure you —**
19   **I want you both to give me the opportunity to meet**
20   **some of your friends, young people in whom I could**
21   **take an interest. New York must be full of them.**
22   **But most of all I want to see you two. I want you to**
23   **feel that this house is your second home.** *(Very*
24   *emotional)* **I will do everything for you. I have no one**
25   **else in the world. I will do everything for you.** *(Again*
26   *she puts her handkerchief to her face.)* **Now I've talked**
27   **a good deal. Have you anything to say to all this?**
28 **LUBBOCK:** *(After rising and taking a few steps about)* **Mrs.**
29   **Mowbrey, I like people who talk frankly, as you do,**
30   **and who go straight to the point. And I'm going to**
31   **be frank with you. There's one big hitch in what**
32   **you propose.**
33 **MRS. MOWBREY: Hitch?**
34 **LUBBOCK: Katy.** *(He looks directly at her and repeats.)*
35   **Katy. Naturally, she wouldn't have anything to say**

1   **about my professional life. — And I want to thank**
2   **you for the confidence you express in my ability to**
3   **be of service to you.** *(He looks up at the ceiling in*
4   *thought.)* **But about those other points: I don't**
5   **know. I tell you frankly, Mrs. Mowbrey, I'm in love**
6   **with Katy. I'm knocked off my feet by Katy. But I**
7   **feel that I don't know her. How can I put it? I'm...**
8   **I'm even afraid of Katy.**
9   **MRS. MOWBREY:** *(Almost outraged)* **What? A man like**
10   **you, afraid of a mere girl!**
11   **LUBBOCK:** *(Short laugh)* **Well, perhaps that's going too**
12   **far; but I swear to you I still can't imagine what it**
13   **will be like to be married to Katy.** *(His manner*
14   *changes and he goes to her briskly as though to shake*
15   *her hand.)* **Really, I think it's best that I say good**
16   **night now. Katy will want to see you alone. So I'll**
17   **thank you very much and say good-bye. And ask if**
18   **I may call on you at some other time.**
19   **MRS. MOWBREY: Nonsense! What possible harm could**
20   **there be — ?** *(The doorbell rings.)* **There! That's the**
21   **doorbell. That's Katy. It's too late to go now. Do**
22   **calm down, Mr. Lubbock.**
23
24
25
26
27
28
29
30
31
32
33
34
35

"In Shakespeare and the Bible" represents Wrath in Thornton Wilder's projected cycle of seven one-act plays depicting The Seven Deadly Sins. It is one of three of the seven that the playwright failed to complete during his lifetime to at least his initial satisfaction. In 1996-1997, F. J. O'Neil constructed two Sins, including "In Shakespeare and the Bible," from the playwright's manuscripts in the Wilder Collection at Yale University. Readers interested in the history of this play are referred to Mr. O'Neil's editorial note on page 192 of *The Collected Short Plays of Thornton Wilder: Volume I* (Theatre Communications Group Press, 1997). This volume also contains extensive information about the history of the cycle and each of its component plays.

Private Eyes

by Steven Dietz

1   Steven Dietz's *Private Eyes* premiered at the Humana Festival
2 of New American Plays at Actors Theatre of Louisville in 1997. The
3 following selection is the opening section of this comic exploration
4 of reality.
5
6
7 **MATTHEW: Next.** *(LISA enters, carrying a shoulder bag.)* **Hello.**
8 **LISA: Hi.**
9 **MATTHEW:** *(Rifling through the resumes)* **You are —**
10 **LISA: Lisa.** *(She hands him her resume.)* **Lisa Foster.**
11 **MATTHEW: Have I seen you before?**
12 **LISA: I don't think so.**
13 **MATTHEW: Your face is awful.**
14 **LISA: Umm, well —**
15 **MATTHEW:** *(Looking at her photo)* **Get a photo that does you**
16   **justice.** *(She stares at him.)* **Well, let's get started.** *(She*
17   *moves to the center of the room. He sits behind the table.)*
18   **You're reading Carol, yes?**
19 **LISA: Yes.**
20 **MATTHEW: Did you have a chance to look at the scene?**
21 **LISA: Yes.**
22 **MATTHEW: Good.**
23 **LISA: From the entrance?**
24 **MATTHEW: Yes.** *(LISA moves to a corner of the room. Looks*
25   *back to MATTHEW.)*
26 **LISA: Is there something that you're looking for?**
27 **MATTHEW: Yes. Whenever you're ready.** *(Pause. Then,*
28   *using her script as a tray, LISA enters the scene. She*
29   *speaks to the unseen customer in the chair.)*
30 **LISA: Hi. What can I get you to drink?** *(Pause)* **Can I start**

1   you off with something from the bar? *(Pause)* **Wine.**
2   *(Pause)* **Beer.** *(Pause)* ***Hello.*** *(Silence)* **Look. Why don't**
3   **I give you a little more time? I have other customers**
4   **who actually take their sunglasses *off* to read the**
5   **menu and actually acknowledge my questions when**
6   **I ask them —** *(Starts off, stops.)* **Oh, god. You're**
7   **Derek Savage — no, right, that's OK, you don't**
8   **have to answer. I understand. They'd mob you in**
9   **here. Oh, god, Mr. Savage, I've seen all your — oh,**
10 **god, I'm saying it. I always thought that if I met you**
11 **I'd have something more original to say than "I've**
12 **seen all your films and I'm a big —" Wow. What?**
13 *(Looks at her script, nods "Yes.")* **Uh-huh.** *(Looks at her*
14 *script, shakes her head "No.")* **Huh-uh.** *(She stares at*
15 *him and then ... blushes ... looks away.)* **Thank you.**
16 **Really. Well ... why don't I give you a little more**
17 **time with the menu and then I'll —** *(Looks at her*
18 *script, shakes her head "No.")* **Huh-uh.** *(Turning the*
19 *page in her script, nods "Yes.")* **Uh-huh.** *(She stares at*
20 *him and then ... slowly covers her mouth with her hand.)*
21 **My, uh, food is up. I need to go and do some, uh,**
22 **waitressing, so —** *(She starts to go, but something he*
23 *has said stops her. She stares at him. She looks over her*
24 *shoulder, around the room. Then she sits in the chair at*
25 *his table, across from him. She extends her hand, and*
26 *"shakes" with the air in front of her.)* **Carol. Carol**
27 **Davis.** *(A pause, then LISA lowers her hand and looks*
28 *up at MATTHEW, expectant. He stares at her.)*
29 MATTHEW: **OK. Good. Thank you, Lisa.** *(He makes some*
30 *notes on a pad in front of him. She waits, hopeful for*
31 *him to say something more — but he does not look up.*
32 *She gathers her things and starts off.)* **Are you in a**
33 **hurry?**
34 LISA: **I thought you were done with me.**
35 MATTHEW: **I'm not done with you. Have you ever**

1   waited tables?

2   LISA: *(Setting her bag down)* **Umm ...**

3   MATTHEW: "Umm." There's no umm here. This is a

4   simple question. Have you waited tables or not?

5   LISA: Well, I —

6   MATTHEW: People think there are things I want to

7   hear. I don't know where they get that notion. I ask

8   direct questions and then watch glaciers form on

9   the faces of people that would eat me alive

10   anywhere else. If we were at a bar and I introduced

11   myself and asked if you'd ever waited tables, you

12   wouldn't hesitate. You wouldn't try to read me for

13   the proper response. You would say yes or no,

14   wouldn't you?

15   LISA: Yes.

16   MATTHEW: And why do we think that is?

17   LISA: Here you have power. Anywhere else you'd have

18   none. *(Silence)*

19   MATTHEW: Let me try this one more time. Have you

20   ever —

21   LISA: No.

22   MATTHEW: Good. Thank you for your honesty.

23   LISA: You're welcome.

24   MATTHEW: Truth is air. And air is precious around here.

25   LISA: Do you want me to do it again?

26   MATTHEW: Oh, yes. And this time I'm looking for a

27   little something more. A stronger relationship

28   between you and Derek Savage. A bit more impact.

29   Don't you think that is needed?

30   LISA: Absolutely.

31   MATTHEW: That's lacking, isn't it?

32   LISA: Yes.

33   MATTHEW: And why do we think that is?

34   LISA: We think maybe because right now he's a chair

35   *(He stares at her.)*

1 MATTHEW: People think I have no sense of humor, but
2   I actually — are you married?
3 LISA: Yes.
4 MATTHEW: But I actually do have a sense of humor. I
5   think humor is vital, life-giving. I think humor is air.
6 LISA: I thought truth was air.
7 MATTHEW: Let's begin.
8 LISA: With the chair again?
9 MATTHEW: Don't you believe you can play a love scene
10   with a chair?
11 LISA: *(Setting her script down)* I should just go —
12 MATTHEW: Don't you believe we project our loved
13   ones? Don't you believe we form a picture in our
14   head and then cast that picture like a shadow onto
15   the person we're with? Don't you think the lover we
16   imagine is actually more real than the one that
17   stands before us?
18 LISA: *(Turning to go)* You're not going to want me in your
19   play.
20 MATTHEW: I want to know this. *(Pause)* Really.
21 LISA: I don't think you're describing love. You're
22   describing vanity. If you'd like me to play the scene
23   as though it were about myself and my image of
24   another person's love for myself, I can do that. But
25   I think that's cheap. And hollow. And utterly
26   insignificant.
27 MATTHEW: But, perhaps that is acting. *(She looks at him,*
28   *hard. Then she walks up very close to him.)*
29 LISA: Acting is the cold hard fact that someone is
30   standing in front of you and you look into their eyes
31   and they want something from you — and you from
32   them — and through some combination of
33   bloodshed and eloquence you find your place with
34   each other. That is acting. What you're describing
35   is one person's ability to manipulate events around

1   them and keep their hands clean in the process.

2   MATTHEW: Doesn't that happen? Haven't you seen that

3   happen?

4   LISA: Yes, I have.

5   MATTHEW: And what would you call that?

6   LISA: **Directing.** *(He stares at her.)*

7   MATTHEW: **I'll read with you.** *(He grabs a script and sits*

8   *in the chair. He takes sunglasses from his pocket and*

9   *puts them on.)* **Whenever you're ready.**

10   LISA: *(Entering)* **Hi. What can I get you to drink?** *(Pause)*

11   **Can I start you off with something from the bar?**

12   *(Pause)* **Wine.** *(Pause)* **Beer.** *(Pause)* **Hello.** *(Beat)*

13   **Look. Why don't I give you a little more time? I**

14   **have other customers who actually take their**

15   **sunglasses *off* to read the menu and actually**

16   **acknowledge my questions when I ask them —**

17   *(Starts off as he removes his sunglasses and looks up at*

18   *her. She stops.)* **Oh, god. You're Derek Savage — no,**

19   **right, that's OK, you don't have to answer. I**

20   **understand. They'd mob you in here. Oh, god, Mr.**

21   **Savage, I've seen all your — oh, god, I'm saying it.**

22   **I always thought that if I met you I'd have**

23   **something more original to say than "I've seen all**

24   **your films and I'm a big —" Wow.**

25   MATTHEW: *(A British accent)* **Welsh.**

26   LISA: **What?**

27   MATTHEW: **Your family. Welsh, a little Scottish, a dash**

28   **of Brit. Close?**

29   LISA: *(Nodding "Yes.")* **Uh-huh.**

30   MATTHEW: **And maybe, way back, some German.**

31   LISA: *(Shaking her head "No.")* **Huh-uh.**

32   MATTHEW: **Well, your ancestors did you proud. You are**

33   **drop-dead gorgeous.**

34   LISA: **Thank you. Really.** *(Pause)* **Well, why don't I give**

35   **you a little time with the menu and then I'll —**

1   **MATTHEW: Are you married?**
2   **LISA:** *(Shaking her head "No.")* **Huh-uh.**
3   **MATTHEW: Boyfriend?**
4   **LISA:** *(Nodding "Yes.")* **Uh-huh.**
5   **MATTHEW: See that he worships you. Settle for**
6   **nothing less.** *(She stares at him, caught in his gaze.)*
7   **LISA: My, uh, food is up. I need to go and do some, uh,**
8   **waitressing, so —**
9   **MATTHEW: Why don't you join me?** *(She stares at him,*
10   *glances around the room.)* **Let people talk. They can't**
11   **touch us.** *(He pulls back her chair from the table and*
12   *she sits. He sits across from her. Extends his hand.)*
13   **Derek. Derek Savage.** *(She shakes it, saying —)*
14   **LISA: Carol. Carol Davis.** *(They hold hands for a moment,*
15   *then MATTHEW pulls away.)*
16   **MATTHEW: Now I believe you.**
17   **LISA: What's that?**
18   **MATTHEW: Now I believe you've never waitressed.** *(He*
19   *quickly returns to his table, shuffles papers.)*
20   **LISA: So, that wasn't what you were looking for?**
21   **MATTHEW: People don't know what they're looking for.**
22   **They just know they're looking. Well, thanks for**
23   **coming in —** *(Reading the name off her resume)* **Lisa.**
24   *(He tosses her resume into the trash can. He speaks,*
25   *brightly.)* **We've done our work. It's lunchtime.**
26   *(Music: "Is You Is or Is You Ain't My Baby?" —*
27   *instrumental break. Lights shift to a Restaurant. A small*
28   *table with two chairs. MATTHEW sits, alone. He lifts a*
29   *menu from the table, looks at it, checks his watch, waits.*
30   *LISA enters, now wearing a waitress apron. She*
31   *stops for a moment when she sees him — then*
32   *approaches the table. She stands near him, pen at the*
33   *ready. Music fades out.)*
34   **LISA: Hi. What can I get you to drink?** *(He looks up, sees*
35   *her.)*

1   MATTHEW: Wait a minute. You said you —
2   LISA: I lied. Something from the bar?
3   MATTHEW: You work here?
4   LISA: Not according to my manager. Do you need a little
5   more time?
6   MATTHEW: I — uh — no. I'm in a hurry.
7   LISA: OK, shoot. *(He stares at her, disbelieving. Then he*
8   *turns to his menu.)*
9   MATTHEW: How's the salmon?
10 LISA: Very good.
11 MATTHEW: And the linguine?
12 LISA: Very good.
13 MATTHEW: I see. What about the veal?
14 LISA: Very good.
15 MATTHEW: I suppose the entire menu is very good.
16 LISA: Yes. Very good.
17 MATTHEW: And would you tell me if something wasn't?
18 LISA: No, I would not.
19 MATTHEW: A good waitress would tell me.
20 LISA: Exactly. Now, what do you want?
21 MATTHEW: Why did you lie to me?
22 LISA: That bugs you.
23 MATTHEW: Of course it does.
24 LISA: Why should it matter if a stranger lies to you?
25 MATTHEW: You're not a stranger.
26 LISA: We've seen each other twice.
27 MATTHEW: In ten minutes.
28 LISA: Let's pick a china pattern. *(She leaves.)*
29 MATTHEW: Hey. I need to order — *(He looks around.*
30   *Looks at his watch. LISA arrives with a glass of red*
31   *wine. Sets it in front of MATTHEW.)* **What's this?**
32 LISA: Our best Merlot.
33 MATTHEW: *(Lifting his menu)* **I'm ready to or —**
34 LISA: *(Taking his menu from him)* **You're in a hurry. I**
35   **ordered for you.**

117

1   MATTHEW: You can't do that.

2   LISA: Sure I can.

3   MATTHEW: Why?

4   LISA: I have power here. Get used to it. *(She stares at him.)*

5   MATTHEW: I'm not in a hurry.

6   LISA: You lied.

7   MATTHEW: I changed my mind.

8   LISA: There's a difference?

9   MATTHEW: Yes.

10   LISA: Do tell.

11   MATTHEW: So, you're married?

12   LISA: Ten minutes ago I was.

13   MATTHEW: And are you still?

14   LISA: More so.

15   MATTHEW: Let me ask you something —

16   LISA: Your food is up. *(She leaves. MATTHEW sips his*

17   *wine. Stares front. Looks around. Looks at his wine.*

18   *Pause. He picks up the small box of matches that is on*

19   *the table. He shakes it and hears nothing, fearing it is*

20   *empty. He opens it and happily discovers that there is*

21   *one match left. He lights it and lets it burn, staring at it.*

22   *Blows it out. Then, using his knife, he scrapes some of*

23   *the charred black match into his wine. He quickly hides*

24   *the burnt match and wipes his knife clean, as LISA*

25   *arrives with a covered food plate. Before she can unveil*

26   *it, MATTHEW lifts his wineglass.)*

27   MATTHEW: I have a problem.

28   LISA: That's obvious.

29   MATTHEW: My wine. It has specks in it. Black specks.

30   I'll need to send it back.

31   LISA: That's our best Merlot.

32   MATTHEW: Specks.

33   LISA: Interesting. Why do we think that is?

34   MATTHEW: I'm Matthew —

35   LISA: I know who you are.

1   MATTHEW: I just wanted to say hello, officially.
2   LISA: *Officially?*
3   MATTHEW: Out of the context of work.
4   LISA: Work?
5   MATTHEW: The audition.
6   LISA: You call that work? You sit there and get paid for
7   having opinions and you call that *work?*
8   MATTHEW: It's what I do.
9   LISA: Believe me. I'd really love to sit here and get paid
10   to tell people whether *I like the way they eat.*
11   Don't have to make the food, don't have to serve
12   it, and don't have to eat it, just speak my mind and,
13   miraculously, day after day, everyone mistakes my
14   *criticism for accomplishment.*
15 MATTHEW: I think you've made your —
16 LISA: *(Sitting in the chair across from him)* "**Frankly, your**
17   **eating just doesn't work for me. I'm looking for**
18   **something more. A stronger relationship between**
19   **you and your breaded chicken. A bit more impact.**
20   **Don't you think that's lacking?**"
21 MATTHEW: I'd like to be alone now.
22 LISA: **Believe me, you are.** *(Referring to the covered plate)*
23   **Careful, that's hot.** *(LISA leaves, taking the wine with*
24   *her. MATTHEW watches her go. He uncovers the plate*
25   *in front of him. The only thing on the plate is a new box*
26   *of matches.*
27   *He smiles a bit. He lifts box and shakes it. It is full.*
28   *Pause. Then, he dumps the matches onto the plate. He*
29   *takes a pen out of his pocket. He writes something inside*
30   *the empty matchbox. He replaces the cover on the plate,*
31   *and sets the matchbox on the table in front of him.*
32   *LISA arrives, carrying a new glass of red wine. She*
33   *sets the wine in front of him.)*
34 LISA: **Here we are. Is everything all right?** *(They stare at*
35   *each other. No shift in tone.)* **Say it.**

119

1 **MATTHEW: No.** *(They stare at each other.)*
2 **LISA: I'm still married.**
3 **MATTHEW: I know that.**
4 **LISA: Are you?** *(MATTHEW slides the matchbox across the*
5   *table, toward her. She looks at him, looks at the*
6   *matchbox, then lifts it. She shakes the box and discovers*
7   *it is empty. She opens the box. She reads the writing in*
8   *the box. She stares at him. Then, she drops the*
9   *matchbox on the table, turns and leaves, quickly, as*
10   *Music plays: "I Want You" by Tom Waits.)*
11 **MATTHEW: Lisa, wait —** *(She is gone. MATTHEW stares*
12   *front. Then he stands, throws a few bills on the table,*
13   *and prepares to go, as LISA reappears. She is wearing*
14   *her coat and carrying her bag. They stand, facing each*
15   *other. Music continues, under.)* **Are we leaving?** *(LISA*
16   *nods.)* **Where are we going?**
17 **LISA: It doesn't matter. We're strangers. Wherever we**
18   **go, we'll be alone.**
19 **MATTHEW: Lisa, I don't know what I'm looking for here —**
20 **LISA: But you know you're looking. Aren't you?** *(She*
21   *walks up very close to him. Looks in his eyes.)* **Do this.**
22 **MATTHEW: What?**
23 **LISA: Lie to everyone but me.** *(They stare at each other.*
24   *Then, they prepare to kiss. As their lips are about to*
25   *come together, ADRIAN's voice is heard from the*
26   *audience.)*
27 **ADRIAN: OK, great, let's take five.**
28
29
30
31
32
33
34
35

Scenes for
Two Females

Cloud Tectonics

by José Rivera

José Rivera's *Marisol* won the 1993 Obie Award for
Outstanding Play. In this selection from *Cloud Tectonics*, which
was first staged during the 1995 Humana Festival of New
American Plays at the Actors Theatre of Louisville, two Latina
women reflect on life in Los Angeles.

CELESTINA: *(Shivering)* **Thank you so much for this.**

**ANÍBAL: Jesus, you're soaked. There's a jacket in the
back seat.**

CELESTINA: *(Putting on jacket)* **Thank you.** *(Short beat)*

**ANÍBAL: I can't believe anyone's out in that deluge.
They're calling it the storm of the century.**

CELESTINA: Where am I?

ANÍBAL: Los Angeles.

CELESTINA: *(Troubled)* **Los Angeles?**

ANÍBAL: Corner of Virgil and Santa Monica.

CELESTINA: *(Means nothing to her.)* **Oh.** *(CELESTINA says
no more. She just rubs her pregnant stomach and stares
ahead. Her silence makes ANÍBAL a little nervous.)*

**ANÍBAL: Can you believe this rain for L.A.? Cool! Raging
floods on Fairfax ... bodies floating down the L.A.
River ... LAX closed ... if the Big One came right
now, forget it, half this city would die. But that's
L.A. for you: disasters just waiting to happen.**
(ANÍBAL laughs. No response from CELESTINA.)

**ANÍBAL: I lived in New York. Lived in every borough
except Staten Island. And Brooklyn. And Queens.
And the thing is, New York kills its people one-by-
one, you know? A gun here, a knife there, hand-to-**

1   hand combat at the ATM, little countable deaths.
2   But this? This L.A. thing? Mass death, mass
3   destruction. One freak flood at the wrong time of
4   year and hundreds die ... the atmosphere sags from
5   its own toxic heaviness and thousands perish ... the
6   Big One is finally born, eats a hundred thousand
7   souls for breakfast. And I'm not even talking fire
8   **season!** *(CELESTINA looks at ANÍBAL for the first time.)*
9   **CELESTINA:** Why don't you go back to New York?
10 **ANÍBAL:** Are you kidding? I love it here.
11
12
13
14
15
16
17
18
19
20
21
22
23
24
25
26
27
28
29
30
31
32
33
34
35

Misreadings

by Neena Beber

1   Nina Beeber's *Misreadings* was part of the Humana Festival of
2 New American Plays at Actors Theatre of Louisville in 1998. It
3 takes place in a college professor's office, minimally represented
4 (just a desk with a tall stack of blue exam composition books on it),
5 and is included here in its entirety.
6
7
8   *Lights up on SIMONE.*
9 **SIMONE: It's important to dress right. I want to look slick.**
10   **To look sleek. To look like a fresh thing. I've got a**
11   **message. I'm the message. Study me, baby, because**
12   **in ten minutes. I'm outta here.** *(SIMONE lights a*
13   *cigarette. Lights up on RUTH.)*
14 **RUTH: What are the issues for which you would kill? I like**
15   **to ask my students this on their first day of class. I**
16   **assign novels where the hero or heroine kills, or is**
17   **killed. I try to bring it home. They tell me they would**
18   **kill to defend their family. They'd kill to defend their**
19   **friends. I ask them if they would kill for their country**
20   **... for their freedom ... what would it take?**
21 **SIMONE: I'd kill for a pair of Prada velvet platforms in**
22   **deep plum. Those are to die for.**
23 **RUTH: Simone. I didn't know what she was doing in my class.**
24   **Neither did she, apparently.** *(To SIMONE)* **Nice segue,**
25   **Simone; would we be willing to die for the same things**
26   **we'd kill for?** *(Out)* **I wanted her to participate. She**
27   **usually sat in the back, never spoke, wore too much**
28   **lipstick and some costume straight out of, what. *Vogue*.**
29   **When she did speak, it was always — disruptive.**
30 **SIMONE: I'd die for love except there ain't no Romeos, not**

125

1   that I've seen; I'd take a bullet for my daddy but
2   he's already dead; I'd die of boredom if it were
3   lethal, but I guess it isn't.
4 RUTH: If I couldn't inspire her, I wanted her gone. I
5   asked her to come to my office hours. I asked her
6   several times. She was failing, obviously. I would
7   have let her drop the class, but it was too late for
8   that. She never bothered to come see me. Not until
9   the day before the final exam. She wanted me to
10   give her a passing grade. *(RUTH turns to SIMONE.)*
11   How can I do that, Simone? You haven't even read
12   the material. Have you read any of the material?
13 SIMONE: I don't find it relevant.
14 RUTH: If you haven't read it, how do you know? You
15   may find yourself surprised. *Anna Karenina* is
16   wonderful.
17 SIMONE: It's long.
18 RUTH: Why not give it a shot?
19 SIMONE: The books you assign are depressing. I don't
20   want to be depressed. Why read stuff that brings
21   you down? Kafka, Jesus Christ — I started it, OK?
22   The guy was fucked up.
23 RUTH: So you were moved at least.
24 SIMONE: Moved to shut the book and find something
25   more interesting to do.
26 RUTH: That's too bad; you might find one of these
27   books getting under your skin, if you stick with it.
28   Haven't you ever read something that's really
29   moved you?
30 SIMONE: Nothing moves me, Dr. Ruth.
31 RUTH: I'm going to have to ask you to put out that
32   cigarette.
33 SIMONE: OK, ask. *(She puts it out.)* See art or be art. I
34   choose the latter.
35 RUTH: Somebody must be paying for this education of

1 yours. I imagine they expect a certain return for
2 their money.
3 SIMONE: How do you know I'm not the one paying for
4 it?
5 RUTH: I don't believe someone who was spending their
6 own money would waste it so flagrantly.
7 SIMONE: OK, Dad chips in.
8 RUTH: Would that be the same father you said was
9 dead?
10 SIMONE: That was a joke or a lie, take your pick.
11 RUTH: You're frustrating the hell out of me, Simone.
12 SIMONE: I don't consider it a waste, you know. I like the
13 socialization part.
14 RUTH: If you fail out of this school, you won't be doing
15 any more "socialization."
16 SIMONE: You assume that I'm failing the others.
17 RUTH: So it's just this class, then? That you have a
18 problem with?
19 SIMONE: Dangling. *(Referring to her grammar)* **Do you**
20 enjoy being a teacher?
21 RUTH: Yes, I do.
22 SIMONE: So I'm paying for your enjoyment.
23 RUTH: It's not a sin to enjoy one's work, Simone.
24 SIMONE: I just don't think you should charge me, if it's
25 more for your pleasure than for mine.
26 RUTH: I didn't say that.
27 SIMONE: Did you ever want to teach at a real school,
28 not some second-rate institution like this?
29 RUTH: I like my job. You're not going to convince me
30 otherwise.
31 SIMONE: Four thousand two hundred and ninety-eight.
32 RUTH: That is — ?
33 SIMONE: Dollars. That's a lot of money. Do you think
34 you're worth it? Do you think this class is worth it?
35 Because I figured it out: this is a four credit class,

1   I broke it down. Four thousand two hundred and
2   ninety-eight. Big ones. Well, do you think that what
3   you have to teach me is worth that? Come on, start
4   talking and we'll amortize for each word.
5 RUTH: You're clearly a bright girl. You can't expect an
6   education to be broken down into monetary terms.
7 SIMONE: You just did. That's a lot of money, right? It's,
8   like, food for a starving family in a fifth-world
9   country for a year at least. It's a car. Well, a used
10   one, anyway. Minus the insurance. Suddenly this
11   number doesn't sound so huge. It's a couple of
12   Armani suits at most. I don't even like Armani. So
13   hey, come on, can't you even say, "Yes, Simone, I am
14   worth two Armani suits. I have that to offer you ..."
15 RUTH: I can't say that, no.
16 SIMONE: No useful skills to be had here.
17 RUTH: The money doesn't go into my pocket, by the
18   way.
19 SIMONE: I think it should. It would be more direct that
20   way; you'd feel more of a responsibility. To me.
21   Personally. Don't you think. Dr. Ruth?
22 RUTH: I'd prefer that you not call me that.
23 SIMONE: But your name is Ruth, and ... you do have a
24   Ph.D., don't you?
25 RUTH: OK, Simone.
26 SIMONE: Wrong kind of doctor, man. All you're
27   interested in is a bunch of books written a hundred
28   years ago, and the books written about those
29   books; you're probably writing a book about a
30   book written about a book right now, am I right?
31 RUTH: If you don't see the connection of books to life,
32   you aren't reading very well. I want you to try. Can
33   you do that? Books might even show you a way to
34   live.
35 SIMONE: I'm already living, Dr. Ruth. Are you? Because

1   it looks like you haven't changed your hairstyle in
2   twenty-five years.
3   RUTH: *(Insulted but covering)* **Well, that's before you were**
4   **born, Simone.**
5   SIMONE: Stuck in your best year? Because I see you in
6   a close-cropped, spiky thing.
7   RUTH: That's enough.
8   SIMONE: And you might want to do something about
9   the way you dress.
10   RUTH: Have you been in therapy?
11   SIMONE: Don't think that's an original suggestion.
12   RUTH: I'm not suggesting anything. I simply want to
13   point out that this is not therapy. I am a teacher,
14   not your therapist. You can't just waltz into my
15   office and say whatever hateful thing you please.
16   SIMONE: I don't know how to waltz.
17   RUTH: I'm giving up here, Simone. You don't like my
18   class, you don't like me, you want to fail out, I can't
19   stop you. *(RUTH goes back to her work. SIMONE does*
20   *not budge. RUTH finally looks up.)* **What?**
21   SIMONE: Drew Barrymore would move me.
22   RUTH: Who?
23   SIMONE: I think Drew would do it. Getting to meet Drew.
24   RUTH: Who's Drew Barrymore?
25   SIMONE: Damn, you really should know these things.
26   She's extremely famous. She's been famous since
27   she was, like, born. I saw her on TV yesterday and
28   she was so real. She connected. You know? You
29   really might relate to your students better if you
30   got a little more up to date.
31   RUTH: You might be right. But you might not be so
32   behind in class if you spent a little less time
33   watching television.
34   SIMONE: Drew is a film star, she's in films. Don't you
35   even go to the movies? Probably only the ones that

1   are totally L-Seven. And I know you don't know
2   what that means. *(She makes an "L" and a "7" with*
3   *her fingers.)* **Square? Anyway, Drew was on TV**
4   because she was being interviewed. They have
5   these daytime talk shows nowadays?
6 RUTH: I've heard of them.
7 SIMONE: And this chick was in the audience and she
8   started to cry. Because she couldn't believe she was
9   there in the same room with Drew, who's been
10   famous forever, right? She was just, like, sitting
11   there sobbing. And this chick, she had her bleached
12   blond hair pasted down real flat, and she was
13   wearing a rhinestone barrette just like Drew used
14   to, but that whole look is so old Drew, so ten-
15   minutes-ago Drew. The new Drew is sleek and
16   sophisticated and coifed and this girl, this girl who
17   wanted to be Drew so bad, she wasn't even current.
18 RUTH: I don't think we're getting anywhere.
19 SIMONE: And that is so sad. Because the thing about
20   Drew is, she is always changing. It's a constant
21   thing with her, the change. And that is, like, what
22   you've got to do ... keep moving or you die. Drew
23   knows that. How to invent yourself again and again
24   so you can keep being someone that you like, the
25   someone that you want to be. And once you're it,
26   you've got to move on. Now where was it you were
27   hoping we'd get to?
28 RUTH: The exam is tomorrow morning at 9 AM. If you
29   read the material, any of the material, I might
30   actually be able to give you a passing grade. But
31   right now I don't think we need to waste any more
32   of each other's time.
33 SIMONE: *(Starts to go.)* You might have said that I go to
34   the movies the way you read books. I would have
35   pointed that out, Dr. Ruth.

1   RUTH: Yes. Well. I suspect we don't think very much
2   alike.
3   SIMONE: A wall between our souls? *(RUTH looks at her,*
4   *about to say something.)* I'm sorry if I've been rude.
5   I'm sure a lot of people like your class. Maybe I
6   wasn't raised well. I'm sure somebody's to blame.
7   *(SIMONE goes to write in a blue exam book.)*
8   RUTH: The next day she showed up at nine on the dot.
9   I felt a certain pride that I had somehow managed
10   to reach her, that she was finally going to make a
11   real effort, bur she handed in her blue book after a
12   matter of minutes. I was rather disgusted and let it
13   sit there, until a pile formed on top of it, a pile of
14   blue books filled with the scrawling, down-to-the-
15   last-second pages of my other more eager, or at
16   least more dutiful, students. Later I began to read
17   them straight through from the top, in the order
18   they were stacked in. I wasn't looking forward to
19   Simone's.
20   In answering my essay question about how the
21   novel *Anna Karenina* moves inevitably toward
22   Anna's final tragic act, my students were, for the
23   most part, thorough and precise. They cited the
24   events that led to Anna's throwing herself in front
25   of the train, touching on the parallel plots and the
26   broader social context. I was satisfied. I felt I had
27   taught well this last semester. My students had
28   learned.
29   In the blue book she had written "All happy
30   people resemble one another, but each unhappy
31   person is unhappy in their own way." So I guess
32   she had read *Anna K*; the opening sentence, at
33   least. My first instinct was to correct the grammar
34   of her little variation. There was nothing else on
35   the page. I flipped through the book; she'd written

1　　　one more line on the last page: "Any world that I'm
2　　　welcome to is better than the one that I come
3　　　from." I'm told it's a rock lyric. Something from the
4　　　seventies. Anna was written in the seventies, too,
5　　　funnily enough, a century earlier.
6　　　　I would have given Simone an F, but I noticed she
7　　　had already marked down the failing grade herself,
8　　　on the back of the book. Or maybe the grade was
9　　　for me.
10　　　　By the time I came to it, days had passed. I didn't
11　　　leap to conclusions. Come to think of it, Anna's
12　　　suicide always takes me by surprise as well, though
13　　　I've read the novel many times and can map its
14　　　inexorable progression. *(SIMONE, just as before …)*
15　SIMONE: That's a lot of money. Do you think you're
16　　　worth it? Do you think this class is worth it? *(RUTH*
17　　　*turns to her, wanting to reach out.)*
18　RUTH: I live in worlds made by words. Worlds where the
19　　　dead can speak, and conversations can be
20　　　replayed, altered past the moment of regret, held
21　　　over and over until they are bent into new
22　　　possibilities.
23　SIMONE: Do you think I'm worth it? Am I? Am I? Am I?
24　RUTH: I live there, where death is as impermanent as an
25　　　anesthesia, and the moment of obliteration is only
26　　　… a blackout. *(SIMONE lights a cigarette as lights*
27　　　*blackout.)*
28　SIMONE: Ten minutes, time's up — told you I'd be gone
29　　　by now, baby. *(The flame illuminates her for a*
30　　　*moment, darkness again.)*
31
32
33
34
35

Scenes for Two Males

Slavs!

by Tony Kushner

1 *Slavs!* is by Tony and Pulitzer Prize winner Tony Kushner.
2
3
4 *In an anteroom outside the Politburo chamber in the*
5 *Hall of the Soviets in the Kremlin. March 1985.*
6 *Smukov and Upgobkin, in suits now, are talking. A*
7 *samovar stands nearby, brewing tea.*
8 VASSILY VOROVILICH SMUKOV: People are not
9 capable of change. They used to be, maybe, but
10 not anymore. In the old days you could ask
11 anything of the people and they'd do it: live
12 without bread, without heat in the winter, take a
13 torch to their own houses, as long as they believed
14 they were building socialism there was no limit to
15 how much they could adapt, transform. Moldable
16 clay in the hands of history.
17 SERGE ESMERELDOVICH UPGOBKIN: And you feel
18 it's different now?
19 VASSILY VOROVILICH SMUKOV: Well, you see. We are
20 all grown less pliable, unsure of our footing,
21 unsure of the way, brittle bones and cataracts ...
22 How are your cataracts, by the way, Serge
23 Esmereldovich?
24 SERGE ESMERELDOVICH UPGOBKIN: Worse, worse.
25 VASSILY VOROVILICH SMUKOV: They should operate.
26 SERGE ESMEKELDOVICH UPGOBKIN: They have.
27 VASSILY VOROVILICH SMUKOV: But ... ?
28 SERGE ESMERELDOVICH UPGOBKIN: But I still have
29 the cataracts.
30 VASSILY VOROVILICH SMUKOV: It grieves me to hear

135

1   that, Serge Esmereldovich.

2 **SERGE ESMERELDOVICH UPGOBKIN:** Old eyes get

3   tough, cloudy. This one *(Points to one eye)* is not

4   really an eye anymore, it's a bottle-cork, it's a

5   walnut. This one *(Points to the other eye)* lets in milky

6   light. I live in a world of milk white ghosts now,

7   luminous beings, washed clean of detail. And I hear

8   better, Vashka: in every voice, a million voices

9   whispering. *(Imitates whispering.)* Sssssshhhhh,

10   shhssshhh ... More tea?

11 **VASSILY VOROVILICH SMUKOV:** No; I'll have to get up

12   to pee in the middle of Aleksii's speech.

13 **SERGE ESMERELDOVICH UPGOBKIN:** Whereas I

14   intend to drink two more cups, so the pressure on

15   my bladder will keep me awake.

16 **VASSILY VOROVILICH SMUKOV:** At least in the bad old

17   days you could sleep through the speeches and not

18   worry that you'd miss a thing. Now the speeches

19   are longer and you have to stay awake to boo. It's

20   miserable: democracy. I am a true apostle of the

21   old scientific creed: Geriatrical materialism. Our

22   motto: Stagnation is our only hope. Our sacred

23   text: silence. Not this interminable debate, blah

24   blah blah, my side, your side — really, this is

25   logorrhea, not revolution.

26 **SERGE ESMERELDOVICH UPGOBKIN:** Patience. There

27   are no shortcuts to the new era. The terrain is vast.

28   Aeons to traverse, everything is implicated,

29   everything encompassed, the world, the universe ...

30   A harsh and unnaturally protracted winter is losing

31   its teeth. A great pressure has built up to this,

32   Vashka, a great public desperation. There is no

33   choice. You'll see that people can change, and change

34   radically. From crown to toe, every cell formed anew.

35   We set the process in motion with our words.

1   VASSILY VOROVILICH SMUKOV: People, I think,
2   would rather die than change.
3   SERGE ESMERELDOVICH UPGOBKIN: Do you really
4   think so? I believe precisely the opposite. We would
5   rather change than die. We have been ordered into
6   motion by history herself, Vashka. When the sun
7   comes out the sky cracks open, the silent flowers
8   twist and sway ...
9
10
11
12
13
14
15
16
17
18
19
20
21
22
23
24
25
26
27
28
29
30
31
32
33
34
35

Below the Belt

by Richard Dresser

1 Richard Dresser's *Below the Belt* premiered in 1995. In the
2 opening scene, two men who are to share a room meet for the
3 first time.
4
5
6 *(In darkness we hear HANRAHAN attempting to type.*
7 *He responds to each keystroke, which echoes in the*
8 *silent room.)*
9 **HANRAHAN: Excellent.** *(Another keystroke)* **Good. Very**
10 **good.** *(Five quick keystrokes)* **Beautiful. *Beautiful.***
11 **Keep it up. Nice and steady.** *(Three quick ones)*
12 **Damn you! Damn you to hell! Bastard!** *(The sound*
13 *of paper being viciously crumpled and another piece of*
14 *paper being put in the typewriter. A pause, then a*
15 *hesitant keystroke.)* **OK, all right, that's the idea.**
16 **Easy does it.** *(The lights slowly come up on*
17 *HANRAHAN's room, which is small and makeshift,*
18 *with two small beds, a simple cooking arrangement, an*
19 *old radio, and a door to the bathroom. HANRAHAN is*
20 *laboriously typing at a desk with a large, old-fashioned*
21 *typewriter. DOBBITT enters, carrying a suitcase. He*
22 *stands there a moment, not wanting to interrupt.*
23 *HANRAHAN doesn't acknowledge him.)*
24 **DOBBITT: I'm Dobbitt.** *(Pause, then louder)* **I'm Dobbitt.**
25 **HANRAHAN:** *(Not looking up)* **Can't you wait 'til I'm**
26 **done?** *(HANRAHAN stares at the typewriter. DOBBITT*
27 *puts his suitcase down as quietly as possible, barely*
28 *making a sound. HANRAHAN turns and glares at him.)*
29 **What's all this ruckus? I'm busy. I'm looking for**
30 **the "y."** *(DOBBITT goes over and hits the "y" on the*

1 typewriter which makes a loud echoing sound.
2 *HANRAHAN stares at DOBBITT.*) **Well, well, well.**
3 **Very impressive. He knows just where they keep**
4 **the "y."** *(HANRAHAN stands up, takes the paper from*
5 *the typewriter, puts it in an envelope, seals the envelope,*
6 *puts the envelope in a manila folder, puts the folder in*
7 *a large envelope which he seals, then puts the large*
8 *envelope in a drawer, which he locks. He puts the key in*
9 *his pocket, which he buttons.)*
10 **DOBBITT: I was just trying to help.**
11 **HANRAHAN: I don't like people looking over my**
12 **shoulder, passing judgment. There's going to be**
13 **trouble if you pry into my affairs. Who are you,**
14 **anyway?**
15 **DOBBITT: I'm Dobbitt. You must be Hanrahan.**
16 **HANRAHAN: I *must* be Hanrahan? I don't have a**
17 **choice?**
18 **DOBBITT: Are you Hanrahan?**
19 **HANRAHAN: Who are you to barge into my room and**
20 **tell me who I must be?**
21 **DOBBITT: You're not Hanrahan?**
22 **HANRAHAN: As it turns out, I *am* Hanrahan, but not**
23 **because it happens to suit your purposes.**
24 **DOBBITT: I'm sorry. It was an endless flight and then**
25 **we drove for hours through the desert. This is**
26 **where they told me to stay.**
27 **HANRAHAN: You're staying here? In my room?**
28 **DOBBITT: It's a two-person room. They told me there**
29 **was someone in here before.**
30 **HANRAHAN: Haney. He left early.**
31 **DOBBITT: Why did he leave? Did something happen?**
32 **HANRAHAN:** *(A long look at DOBBITT)* **Which bed?**
33 **DOBBITT: Oh, it doesn't matter.**
34 **HANRAHAN: Yes it does. This one in the corner gets an**
35 **icy wind off the desert snapping right through it.**

1   The window doesn't close. A man could freeze to
2   death in this bed.
3   DOBBITT: If it's all the same to you, I'll take the other
4   bed.
5   HANRAHAN: Suit yourself. *(DOBBITT throws his suitcase*
6   *down on the bed and starts unpacking. HANRAHAN*
7   *pours himself a mug of coffee.)* That one's a
8   sweatbox. Right next to the radiator, which clangs
9   in your ear like a train wreck all night long. You'll
10   be begging for mercy by morning.
11   DOBBITT: Why don't we move the beds?
12   HANRAHAN: That's an idea. That should solve
13   everything. *(DOBBITT tries to move the bed.)* Except
14   they're bolted to the floor. Lots of thievery on the
15   compound.
16   DOBBITT: They're stealing beds?
17   HANRAHAN: Not since the bolts went in.
18   DOBBITT: Which bed do you sleep in?
19   HANRAHAN: Both. I start in the one next to the window.
20   When I start to freeze I climb in the other one. Then,
21   when I can't breathe I get up and start the day. I
22   guess that's all gone now that *you're* here.
23   DOBBITT: I seem to have caught you at a bad time.
24   HANRAHAN: Oh?
25   DOBBITT: I fear I've upset you.
26   HANRAHAN: *You've* upset me? That's a bit grandiose,
27   don't you think?
28   DOBBITT: You seem disgruntled.
29   HANRAHAN: Gruntled or disgruntled, it has nothing to
30   do with you. *(DOBBITT watches HANRAHAN sipping*
31   *from a cup. He yawns.)*
32   DOBBITT: Is that coffee?
33   HANRAHAN: Yes. *(HANRAHAN doesn't move.)*
34   DOBBITT: I feel as though I've been traveling forever. I
35   should either sleep or try to revive myself. If there's

1   any more coffee.
2   HANRAHAN: There's plenty more coffee. *(HANRAHAN*
3   *still doesn't move.)*
4   DOBBITT: I could get it myself.
5   HANRAHAN: Are you asking for coffee?
6   DOBBITT: Only if it's no bother.
7   HANRAHAN: Well of course it's a bother! *(HANRAHAN*
8   *angrily starts clattering around the coffee pot.)*
9   DOBBITT: Then please, forget it.
10   HANRAHAN: Now that I'm knee-deep in it you don't
11   want any?
12   DOBBITT: If it's easier to continue ...
13   HANRAHAN: *(Turning on him)* See here. I'm not a puppet
14   on a string. You'll have to make up your mind and
15   you'll have to do it right now.
16   DOBBITT: No coffee. I don't want to put you out.
17   HANRAHAN: I'm already put out. The only question is
18   whether or not you want coffee.
19   DOBBITT: Everything else being equal, I would say yes
20   to coffee.
21   HANRAHAN: Very well. *(He pours a cup of coffee.)* It just
22   means I have to make a whole new pot for myself.
23   *(He hands it to DOBBITT who tries to refuse the coffee.)*
24   DOBBITT: Then you take this, please —
25   HANRAHAN: No!
26   DOBBITT: I insist! *(As they struggle, the coffee spills on*
27   *HANRAHAN, who bellows.)* My God! I'm terribly
28   sorry —
29   HANRAHAN: Look what you've done!
30   DOBBITT: It was an accident —
31   HANRAHAN: If you'd made up your mind this never
32   would have happened. *(HANRAHAN dries himself*
33   *with a towel. There's a beep from a small intercom on*
34   *the wall. HANRAHAN stops and glares at it.)* Well.
35   That's Merkin. And he sounds upset. *(Grimly)* Come

1   **on, Dobbitt, it's time to meet the boss.**
2   *(HANRAHAN hurries from the room with DOBBITT*
3   *following as lights fade.)*
4
5
6
7
8
9
10
11
12
13
14
15
16
17
18
19
20
21
22
23
24
25
26
27
28
29
30
31
32
33
34
35

Scenes for
One Female
and Two Males

Porno

by Mario Fratti

1   Among the awards won by Mario Fratti's *Nine* were the O'Neill
2   Selection Award, Richard Rodgers Award, Outer Critics Circle
3   Award, eight Drama Desk awards, and five Tony Awards. *Porno*,
4   included here in its entirety, is about how the past and the present
5   collide in a marriage.

6

7

8   *(DORINE is alone at home; she is watching television. We*
9   *see DICK in a telephone booth dialing a number; the*
10   *telephone rings in DORINE's apartment.)*
11 **DORINE:** *(Picking up the receiver)* **Hello?**
12 **DICK: Dorine?**
13 **DORINE: Yes ...**
14 **DICK: Are you alone? Can you talk?**
15 **DORINE: Who is it?**
16 **DICK: It's Dick.**
17 **DORINE: Dick who?**
18 **DICK: Dick Raffert ... Don't you remember me?**
19 **DORINE.** *(After a brief pause)* **I'm sorry, no.**
20 **DICK: Dick ... May 1982 ...**
21 **DORINE: I'm sorry but ... how am I supposed to remember**
22   **someone I met in '82? And with a name like yours. I**
23   **must have met at least ten ...**
24 **DICK: Not like me, I hope, not intimately like me.**
25 **DORINE: Listen, I am very busy and can't —**
26 **DICK:** *(Interrupting)* **I know you're pretending. I'm sure you**
27   **remember me ... Dick, the man you loved with such**
28   **passion and generosity ...**
29 **DORINE:** *(Skeptically, ironically)* **Me? Passion and generosity?**
30 **DICK: Do you want to deny it now?**

1   DORINE: Listen, either you got the wrong number or
2   you feel like joking. Sir, please let me —
3   DICK: *(Interrupting)* So formal with me, after what we ...
4   DORINE: Excuse me but I don't know you, I don't
5   remember you. Honestly!
6   DICK: In '82 ... 54th Street ... third floor ... no elevator
7   ... *(A silence)*
8   DORINE: *(Perhaps remembering now)* Third floor ...
9   DICK: You remember now? Narrow, dirty stairs ...
10 DORINE: *(Vaguely)* Maybe, it's possible. Everything is
11   possible. Listen. Dick, I'm married now. To a man I
12   love. We're happy. Thank you for calling, good night.
13 DICK: No, no, wait ... You must first remember who I
14   am. It's impossible you've forgotten me.
15 DORINE: *(To end the conversation)* Listen, Dick, I
16   remember everything. You were great! You are ...
17   special, unique. A real master. It was a great
18   pleasure to know you. I have pleasant memories of
19   you, wonderful memories. Good night!
20 DICK: I never forgot you.
21 DORINE: That makes me happy. Thanks for the
22   compliment. Good night!
23 DICK: No ... You must first prove that you at least
24   remember what we did together. Those precious
25   hours ...
26 DORINE: Crazy years. What we did was probably
27   foolish.
28 DICK: Probably?
29 DORINE: Sure! For sure!
30 DICK: Tell me what we did together.
31 DORINE: What do you want? A list? I don't keep
32   records. I don't take notes, I don't remember every
33   detail. Please ...
34 DICK: To be sure that you remember me, describe what
35   we did together with a single word — four letters —

1   only four — one, two, three, four ... It's easy, isn't it?
2   DORINE: *(Thinking, without understanding what he is*
3   *alluding to)* **Fine. We even did that. So what?**
4   DICK: **We made an F-I-L-M. We made a film together!**
5   DORINE: *(Who has finally understood)* **Ah. You are the**
6   **one who ... Forgive me. They didn't introduce us. I**
7   **didn't remember your name. Forgive me.**
8   DICK: **"Burning Lips" — remember? A nice little film. I**
9   **had almost forgotten it, but today I saw it again**
10   **and ... you and me together ... Dorine, I have never**
11   **met a woman more ... sensual than you ...**
12   **generous, passionate, a real woman ... I was very**
13   **excited when I saw again how you —**
14   DORINE: *(Interrupting, worried by this news)* **Where did**
15   **you see it? They promised me that they would**
16   **destroy it!**
17   DICK: **And you trusted that low-life director?**
18   DORINE: **He swore to me he would! A few copies in the**
19   **Orient were impossible to get back. Japan, Hong**
20   **Kong, and Taiwan. In America, not a single copy!**
21   **All destroyed!**
22   DICK: **I saw it half an hour ago and my desire came**
23   **back. You are fantastic. The best in the world! If**
24   **you are alone, I'll come to your place and —**
25   DORINE: **No, no! I'm happily married. My husband is**
26   **coming back any minute! Please! We get along.**
27   **Don't ruin everything with ...** *(She hesitates; she is*
28   *undecided and confused.)* **Where did you see it? Tell**
29   **me. Please ...**
30   DICK: **I enjoyed every moment of it, horny with desire.**
31   **You bring real passion to it. Your husband is a**
32   **lucky man. Do you do to him what you did to me**
33   **when —**
34   DORINE: **Where did you see it? I even paid that**
35   **bastard. Five hundred dollars, so they would**

1   destroy every copy.
2 DICK: Five hundred! They only gave us one hundred to
3   make the film. At least to me. And you ... How
4   much did they give you?
5 DORINE: Me too, just one hundred. I was broke then. I
6   had to pay rent. Then things got better. Now I'm all
7   right. Tell me where ... I have some money now. We
8   can buy it back.
9 DICK: "We?" Together? Together again?
10 DORINE: No, please ... The past is past. I am older now,
11   I am wiser.
12 DICK: More experienced, more passionate. A real woman.
13 DORINE: Where? Give me the address. I'll go there
14   tomorrow and offer to buy it.
15 DICK: I already asked the lady in charge.
16 DORINE: What lady? Who is she?
17 DICK: She owns the place where I saw the film. I wanted
18   a copy for me, to re-live those moments a hundred
19   times. She doesn't want to sell it.
20 DORINE: Why? Where is she? Is she the manager of a
21   movie theatre? Perhaps they'll show it for a few
22   days and then ...
23 DICK: She told me it's part of a cycle.
24 DORINE: What cycle?
25 DICK: A tape that lasts twenty-four hours. Twenty films
26   put together, showed continuously.
27 DORINE: Where?
28 DICK: In this place.
29 DORINE: What place?
30 DICK: Private.
31 DORINE: What is it? A movie theatre? A club?
32 DICK: A club, in a certain sense; very private.
33 DORINE: Who goes there? What type of an audience?
34 DICK: Men, women ...
35 DORINE: What kind of women? Why do they want to

1   watch films like that?
2   DICK: They don't watch them, really ... They just create
3   atmosphere.
4   DORINE: Atmosphere?
5   DICK: Background, while the couples ...
6   DORINE: Couples? What kind of place is it? Where is it?
7   DICK: At 40th Street. I went there a couple of times.
8   And I noticed, this time I noticed ... When I saw
9   myself again — on the screen ...
10 DORINE: What screen?
11 DICK: A T.V., screen ... a V.C.R. I told my — *(He*
12   *hesitates; regretting having said so much.)*
13 DORINE: "My" — who?
14 DICK: ... a dear friend. You don't go to those places
15   alone. I told her: "Watch, watch Dorine. Watch and
16   learn." And I have to tell the truth. You women
17   have a spirit of competition. She tried to imitate
18   you, she tried her best, but no one is as good as
19   you, Dorine. Are you still called Dorine or have you
20   changed your name?
21 DORINE: *(Ignoring him)* Then that place is a kind of ...?
22 DICK: Hotel for ... "affectionate friendships."
23 DORINE: A whore house.
24 DICK: In a broad sense ... There aren't any women. You
25   bring the woman yourself ... They offer only pink
26   lights, a bed, two towels, television that runs
27   constantly ... And you were there, fresh as a rose,
28   horny as a tigress. But your moans, were they real
29   or for the director? For the audience? I've never
30   understood: We never understand with you women.
31 DORINE: What kind of place? Elegant? Expensive? What
32   kind of clientele?
33 DICK: Modest. Medium price. Managers with
34   secretaries, mature women with studs. I was
35   surprised to see such couples. Middle-aged women

1   begin to like young boys. And they pay for the
2   room. Of course. Your husband, how old is he? I'm
3   still in good shape. Thirty-six. One night with me,
4   Dorine, and you'll feel like —
5   DORINE: *(Interrupting)* What's the exact address?
6   DICK: Between the fifties and the thirties. Give me
7   another opportunity, Dorine, and —
8   DORINE: No. Give me the exact address.
9   DICK: I'll give it to you when we see each other. I have
10   an idea. We'll get together there, take a room and
11   ... try to recreate the film, the same energy, the
12   same enthusiasm. It would be an original
13   experience, unique. In life, before television, how
14   many people had the chance to repeat — in front of
15   a video — the unique situation, we are unique, you
16   and I! No one, I bet! A perfect couple!
17   DORINE: Forget the past, please, and help me.
18   DICK: *(Gallantly)* At your service, my love!
19   DORINE: Don't joke around. For the sake of the past, of
20   what we did and enjoyed together —
21   DICK: Enjoyed? Then you really had orgasms!
22   DORINE: Yes ... We were young, it was a beautiful,
23   healthy experience.
24   DICK: But you ignored me immediately, after, as soon
25   as we were through. Why?
26   DORINE: A habit ... Just like great actors. They kiss in
27   front of the camera. And then — "bye bye!" ... As
28   if they hadn't even met. I wanted to separate my
29   screen life from my real life.
30   DICK: *(With desire)* Let's return to reality. After having
31   seen that film, I have to do it with you again. I need
32   you! *(With desire)* Dorine, I want to give you the best
33   I ever —
34   DORINE: *(Interrupting, pretending that her husband has
35   arrived)* My husband! He's at the door! Give me your

1   **number, right away! I'll call you tomorrow!**

2 **DICK:** *(Uncertain)* **But I ...**

3 **DORINE: Right away, he's opening the door! I'm**

4   **hanging up!**

5 **DICK:** *(Rapidly)* **My home number is 242-3317!**

6   *(Repeating, clearly)*

7   *(DORINE hangs up. DICK does too, deep in thought. A*

8   *brief blackout indicates the passage of time.)*

9

10   *(A few days later. DORINE is wearing a different dress.*

11   *She is reading. PAUL, her husband, enters. His steps are*

12   *slow and measured. He stares at her a long time, with*

13   *hatred.)*

14 **DORINE:** *(Timidly, affectionately)* **Do you want a cup of**

15   **coffee?** *(PAUL comes forward, furious. He stares at her.*

16   *He takes the book. He reads the title. He throws it away.*

17   *He bangs on the table, furious. With rage he destroys*

18   *several objects. DORINE is frightened.)*

19 **DORINE: What happened? What's the matter with you?**

20   **Did they fire you?**

21 **PAUL: Yeah, sure! So you would starve! You deserve it!**

22 **DORINE: Why? What's happened? What have I done?**

23 **PAUL: You were used to it, weren't you? When you were**

24   **an actress — off, off — where I had the misfortune**

25   **of finding you. You told me that they didn't pay**

26   **you. Real starvation!**

27 **DORINE: Difficult times. But please, calm down. Tell me**

28   **what happened!**

29 **PAUL: I saw you the first time, in that play ... at the**

30   **Café ...**

31 **DORINE: Café La Mama ... "Madame Senator."**

32 **PAUL: You were one of the whores.**

33 **DORINE: A role like any other. Completely dressed,**

34   remember? It was a musical. A political musical.

35 **PAUL: Political, yes. It was about how to screw the next**

1   guy. In what other plays have you ... performed?

2   **DORINE:** *(Running to a drawer which she opens)* **I have all**

3   **the programs.** *(She takes them and shows them.)* **Off-**

4   **off ... little theatres, clubs, schools ...**

5   **PAUL: And they never paid you, eh?**

6   **DORINE: Seldom. Actors aren't paid in New York, you**

7   **know that.**

8   **PAUL: How did you live? How did you pay your bills?**

9   **DORINE: Waitressing in several restaurants, remember?**

10   **You even came as a customer to the "Three Fools" ...**

11   **PAUL: I'm the fool.**

12   **DORINE: You didn't pay. You were a guest ... They told**

13   **me that you could eat there for free, now and then.**

14   **PAUL: Who told you?**

15   **DORINE: The owner.**

16   **PAUL: A friend of yours? An intimate friend? A lover?**

17   **DORINE: Oh no! A good man. In love with his wife.**

18   **Deeply in love.**

19   **PAUL: Did you have an agent, for your ... theatrical**

20   **enterprises?**

21   **DORINE: It's difficult to find an agent. Only if you're**

22   **well known.**

23   **PAUL:** *(Staring at her, ironical)* **What a pity!** *(Slowly)*

24   **Perhaps he would have found you a chance to ...**

25   **make some films.** *(A silence; they stare at each other.)*

26   **How many films have you made?**

27   **DORINE:** *(Vague, uncertain)* **One ... a silly college film.**

28   **PAUL: What part did you play?**

29   **DORINE: One of the students.**

30   **PAUL: And what did this student do? Go to bed with the**

31   **professor?**

32   **DORINE: Oh no! There were six or seven of us, at a party.**

33   **PAUL: What kind of party?**

34   **DORINE: A family get-together.**

35   **PAUL: What kind of family get-together? An orgy?**

1   DORINE: No ... But why are you asking me all these
2   questions?
3   PAUL: ... I am curious about your ... "movie career."
4   DORINE: All of a sudden?
5   PAUL: *(Breaking something else in rage)* **Yes, yes, all of a**
6   **sudden. You never spoke to me about it. You never**
7   **told me anything! How many men have been in**
8   **your life! You never told me!**
9   DORINE: We decided not to keep stupid lists. My past
10   and your past don't count. We were reborn when
11   we met and fell in love.
12   PAUL: Very convenient, my friend. *(Correcting himself)*
13   Too convenient, *enemy* of my life!
14   DORINE: Men generally have a past that's more ...
15   intense. Dozens of women in your life, I'm sure.
16   We, instead ...
17   PAUL: We who?
18   DORINE: We women. Two or three mistakes. Sweethearts
19   who deceived us, betrayed us, abandoned us.
20   PAUL: How many?
21   DORINE: I told you ... Three ... But why dig up the past?
22   PAUL: Because I want to know!
23   DORINE: Really? All of a sudden? What happened? Who
24   have you seen?
25   PAUL: No one.
26   DORINE: Strange ... You have never come home this
27   furious. You must have seen someone, there must
28   be a reason ...
29   PAUL: There is a reason, but first ... first I want the
30   truth from you! The absolute truth! How many
31   films have you made?
32   DORINE: ... Only that one ... a big nothing of a film.
33   PAUL: How come you never showed it to me?
34   DORINE: It was destroyed, burnt. There are no copies
35   around.

1   **PAUL: Oh yeah? Are you sure? No copies! And what do**
2   **you know about it? They make thousands of copies**
3   **of films like that!** *(A silence; they stare at each other.)*
4   **You're not saying anything? Why don't you admit it**
5   **was porno? That guy with you, the one you did ...**
6   **things with, was he one of your three lovers?** *(A*
7   *silence)*
8   **DORINE:** *(Staring at him)* **Where did you see it?**
9   **PAUL: See what?**
10 **DORINE: A porno film where you think you recognized**
11   **me —**
12 **PAUL:** *(Furious, interrupting)* **Recognize? What gall!** *(He*
13   *follows her because he would like to hit her.)* **You are**
14   **there, with everything ... open, wide open —**
15   **obscenely!**
16 **DORINE:** *(Calmly; by now she knows that her husband has*
17   *seen the film in the "club.")* **Where did you see it?**
18   **Show it to me.**
19 **PAUL: Why? You never saw it? Weren't you curious to**
20   **see yourself in action?**
21 **DORINE: Where did you see it?**
22 **PAUL: "Where" is not important. What counts is the fact**
23   **that the film exists and that you are *admitting* you**
24   **made it; it's you in that ... incredible garbage!**
25 **DORINE: I don't admit anything. I want to see it with**
26   **you.**
27 **PAUL: Are you crazy? That's absurd. How could I show**
28   **up in that place with you, my wife, and ... we watch**
29   **it together ... among so many? ...**
30 **DORINE: So many what?**
31 **PAUL: ... Degenerates who go to see that type of ...**
32 **DORINE: Just you and me. We'll see it alone, you and**
33   **me, privately.** *(A brief silence; PAUL is perplexed.)*
34   **Let's go. If it's someone who looks like me ...**
35 **PAUL:** *(Furious again)* **It's you! It's you! And you know it**

1   perfectly well!

2   DORINE: *(Calmly, continuing)* **We'll buy the film, we'll**

3   **buy it back.**

4   PAUL: **And will those people sell it to you? Should I buy**

5   **it back and pay for what you ... for those horrible**

6   **scenes?**

7   DORINE: **No. I will. After we've seen it together, we'll**

8   **tell the owner of this ... place that ... Either he sells**

9   **it or we sue.**

10   PAUL: **"*We* sue?"**

11   DORINE: **I have my father's inheritance now. I can sue,**

12   **demand, buy.**

13   PAUL: **Look at your gall! Instead of weeping, being**

14   **ashamed, sorry and asking for forgiveness.**

15   DORINE: **Me? For what?**

16   PAUL: **For what you've done! For your horrible past!**

17   DORINE: *(Stares at him calmly.)* **Let's go and see this film,**

18   **first. Then we'll talk about it.**

19   PAUL: *(Hesitant)* **It's a depressing, squalid place. It isn't**

20   **for women like you ...**

21   DORINE: **Oh yes?** *(Ironically)* **One of those dark, dingy**

22   **little places where men go, alone and desperate, to**

23   **watch the flesh market!**

24   PAUL: **Flesh market. Exactly! You know what I'm talking**

25   **about. When I saw my wife doing such horrible**

26   **things ... I wanted to kill you!**

27   DORINE: **Did you tell anyone?**

28   PAUL: **Who? I was ashamed, I felt like a criminal! And**

29   **the criminal was you! The culprit was you!**

30   DORINE: *(Calm, vaguely ironic)* **Did you tell this person,**

31   **this friend of yours — generally one goes to the**

32   **movies with someone — did you tell *him*, this**

33   **friend of yours, that woman looked like your wife?**

34   PAUL: **Never! One doesn't tell a thing like to anyone!**

35   DORINE: **Not even to your friend? Your intimate friend?**

1 PAUL: No.

2 DORINE: Who is he? Do I know him?

3 PAUL: No! No one you know!

4 DORINE: So much the better. Otherwise, he too would
5   have thought that the actress looked like me.

6 PAUL: Actress? What actress? That was a whore! And
7   how she enjoyed it, that whore, the ... *(Refrains; he*
8   *is furious.)* what she had in her mouth. *(He is ready to*
9   *hit her again.)*

10 DORINE: *(Calm)* Let's go see this film. You made me
11   curious.

12 PAUL: You've really got nerve. You know perfectly well
13   what I am talking about and you are pretending to ...

14 DORINE: I'm not pretending anything. But *I know*
15   *perfectly well* what you are talking about.

16 PAUL: *(Confused)* So? ... You're admitting?

17 DORINE: First I have to see it together with you. Let's go.

18 PAUL: *(Who obviously does not want to go to the "club")*
19   First you have to tell me that you are the
20   protagonist of *Burning Lips.*

21 DORINE: Did you see my name in the credits?

22 PAUL: No. I missed them. I never read them.

23 DORINE: Didn't you watch the beginning again, after
24   the shock, out of curiosity, to see the name of the
25   actress?

26 PAUL: No ... it's one of those places where ... the film
27   isn't shown again right away ... It's a tape on a VCR
28   that lasts twenty-four hours.

29 DORINE: *(Feigning surprise)* Twenty-four hours? What
30   time did you see it? We'll go back around that time
31   and see it from the beginning. With the titles, the
32   credits ...

33 PAUL: I don't remember ...

34 DORINE: At lunchtime? You often leave the office for a
35   couple of hours ...

1   PAUL: Perhaps ...

2   DORINE: Let's go at lunchtime then. *(She takes the*

3   *newspaper; consults the movie schedule.)* **What's the**

4   **name of that movie theatre? Is it near your office?**

5   PAUL: Those obscene little places are not listed.

6   DORINE: What's the address?

7   PAUL: *(Vague)* A side street near Third Avenue.

8   DORINE: Fiftieth? Fortieth? Thirtieth?

9   PAUL: *(Vague)* Between fiftieth and thirtieth.

10 DORINE: Around fortieth?

11 PAUL: Around there.

12 DORINE: Fine. Let's go there.

13 PAUL: *(Trying to avoid it)* All right. If you admit that ...

14   you were in that film, and if you tell me that you

15   are ashamed and sorry ...

16 DORINE: *(Firmly)* I don't admit anything. I am not

17   ashamed. I am not sorry. First I want the facts.

18   Let's examine the facts

19 PAUL: *(Furious again)* I'm going to kill you! You women

20   are incredible! Even when you are guilty, caught

21   with your hands in the till, or in this case with —

22   Let's forget it — You women manage to turn the

23   tables. I'm becoming the defendant now!

24 DORINE: Exactly.

25 PAUL: What do you mean by that?

26 DORINE: Nothing ...

27 PAUL: No, explain yourself.

28 DORINE: Only that you shouldn't accuse anyone

29   without proof.

30 PAUL: More proof than this? No one ever had more

31   proof than me! It's ... "Visual" proof. A movie with

32   incredible details; close-ups of morbid, clinical

33   obscenity. It made me vomit.

34 DORINE: Fine. Let's go see it.

35 PAUL: *(Pretending to "suffer")* I can't, I can't ... It would

1   **hurt too much ... It's a disgusting spectacle. I can't**
2   **see it again but I am ready to forgive you if ...**
3 **DORINE: Forgive me for what?**
4 **PAUL: For your horrible past! I should torture you, beat**
5   **you up, kill you, throw you out of the house, and**
6   **instead it's me who ...**
7 **DORINE: Who ... ?**
8 **PAUL: ... Who is almost apologizing.**
9 **DORINE: If someone doesn't have proof, he has to**
10   **apologize.**
11 **PAUL:** *(Incredulous, astonished)* **Are you serious? Should I**
12   **"apologize" and ask to be forgiven?**
13 **DORINE: Exactly.**
14 **PAUL: For what?**
15 **DORINE: You know.**
16 **PAUL: What are you talking about?**
17 **DORINE: Apologize and perhaps, if I think you are**
18   **sincere, I will forgive you, I am ready to forgive you.**
19 **PAUL: You mean you're ready to die!**
20 **DORINE:** *(Calm)* **I said — to forgive you. We women**
21   **know how to understand and forgive.**
22 **PAUL:** *(Exploding)* **Bitch! Slut! Whore! First you do those**
23   **things, in a film seen by millions of people. Your ...**
24   **parts exposed to the world, forever. And then you**
25   **want me to apologize! This is the last straw! Out!**
26   **Out of my house!**
27 **DORINE:** *(Very calm)* **Yes, I'm getting out.** *(Puts on a*
28   *jacket; takes her purse, ready to leave; she speaks*
29   *slowly, with great clarity.)* **I ... "betrayed" you, as you**
30   **say, years ago, before I met you. You betrayed me**
31   **...** ***today.*** *(She goes out, leaving him astonished.)*
32 **PAUL:** *(To himself, incredulous)* ***Today? How does she***
33   ***know? How did she find out?*** *(Immobility. Blackout.*
34   *Curtain.)*
35

And Palm-Wine Will Flow

by Bole Butake

1   Bole Butake is one of Cameroon's leading playwrights. This
2 selection, taken from his best-known drama, *And Palm-Wine Will
3 Flow*, reflects traditional West African reactions to a time of
4 historical transition. *And Palm-Wine Will Flow* had its grand
5 premiere in the Amphi 700 of the University of Yaounde on March
6 27, 1990, in the presence of Mr. John Niba Ngu, the Honorable
7 Minister of Agriculture. The cast was as follows:

8
9 **DRAMATIS PERSONAE**
10   In order of appearance
11   **SHEY NGONG**   Chief priest of Nyombom
12   **NSANGONG**   Friend of Shey Ngong
13   **MESSENGER**   From the palace
14   **EARTH-GODDESS**
15   **VOICE**

16
17 **SETTING:** *Ewawa, imaginary Fondom (chiefdom) in the*
18   *grasslands.*
19   *The sacred grove of Nyombom, characterized by an*
20   *elaborately decorated pot "nshaan wong" in which libation*
21   *is poured to the gods. Elsewhere in the grove are a number*
22   *of masks, also elaborately decorated with dark fibre or*
23   *cloth, thus making them easy to be used as disguises by*
24   *various characters in the play. Other prominent features of*
25   *the grove are a gourd and a sacred gong. All action takes*
26   *place in the same place.*
27 **VOICE:** *(Off-stage)* **Shey Ngong, are you not coming to the**
28   **palace? Where are you going to when all roads are**
29   **leading to the palace?**
30 **SHEY NGONG:** *(Making entrance)* **Is there any thing of**

161

1   import, apart from the merrymaking? I am going to

2   the grove for some peace.

3   VOICE: But Shey, do you or do you not know that

4   Kibanya is receiving the red feather today from the

5   sacred hands of the Fon himself?

6   SHEY NGONG: So I have heard.

7   VOICE: And palm-wine will flow as usual. Come with me

8   to the palace, Shey. The Fon will not take your

9   absence kindly.

10   SHEY NGONG: I am going to the grove. My obligation is

11   to the gods of the land. My duty is to the gods. Not

12   to the Fon and palm-wine.

13   VOICE: Swallow your words, Shey! The cockroach does

14   not call a fowl to a wrestling match. It is a foolish

15   rat that argues with the cat.

16   SHEY NGONG: So I am the rat? I am the cockroach?

17   You knave. The gorilla can do nothing to an iroko

18   tree.

19   VOICE: Eh? You are the iroko tree, are you? I see you

20   want to wrestle with the father and owner of this

21   land of Ewawa.

22   SHEY NGONG: Eh? Who owns the land? Because he

23   takes what belongs to the land and no one lifts a

24   finger?

25   VOICE: Swallow your words, Shey. I say swallow your

26   words.

27   SHEY NGONG: I will not. I am the cockroach. A gorilla

28   can do nothing to the iroko tree.

29   VOICE: Shey Ngong, you will be hearing from the palace

30   before the sun goes down.

31   SHEY NGONG: Away you fawning, stooging dog! Away

32   to your lord and drown yourselves in palm-wine.

33   What a land!

34   VOICE: Shey, I have already warned. You will be hearing

35   from the palace before the sun goes to sleep.

1   SHEY NGONG: And palm-wine will flow.
2   VOICE: You said it. And palm-wine will flow! Palm-wine
3   will flow! You just wait and see. Palm-wine will
4   flow.
5   SHEY NGONG: What a land! What a people! And to
6   think that people in other lands ... What a people!
7   *(Moves over to the sacred pot from which he takes out*
8   *the sacred honey and pours some wine into it from the*
9   *gourd.)*
10   Oh! Nyombom!
11   Creator and guardian of the land,
12   And you our illustrious forebears,
13   Grant me strength and wisdom
14   To weather the surging storm.
15   The Fon has lost vision.
16   The noble men and elders of this land
17   Now listen only to the inner voice
18   Of greed, and fear of a man who has
19   Surrounded himself with listeners
20   And watchdogs to do his bidding.
21   Nyombom and you, ancestors,
22   Grant me strength and wisdom
23   Grant me patience and love ...
24   *(His invocation is interrupted by the rising sound of*
25   *distant music and loud applause and ululations.)*
26   Kibanya must be receiving his red feather now.
27   From today he will stand in the market place
28   and beat his chest and speak in a loud voice.
29   The land! The land! What a people!
30   NSANGONG: *(Off-Stage)* Shey, can I come? Or shall I
31   wait outside? The load that I am carrying must be
32   put down.
33   SHEY NGONG: Come inside then. Come. This place is
34   cool and peaceful; especially for one carrying a
35   load. Come.

1   NSANGONG: *(Making entrance)* **The place is really cool —**
2   **eh? It is a boiling pot out there.**
3   SHEY NGONG: **Where are you coming from; so agitated**
4   **like a monkey that has missed the hunter's bullet?**
5   NSANGONG: **I am just from the palace and ...**
6   SHEY NGONG: **You must have missed the crowning**
7   **moment. What did you go there for?**
8   NSANGONG: **Shey, listen to me and stop your rambling.**
9   **The Fon is mad at you and has sworn ...**
10 SHEY NGONG: **That I will hear from him before the sun**
11   **goes to sleep. Not so?**
12 NSANGONG: **So you know already? Did the tortoise really**
13   **beat the hare in the racing match? Where is he?**
14 SHEY NGONG: **No. No tortoise has beaten the hare.**
15   **Only that Kibanya's shadow and one of the Fon's**
16   **watchdogs wandered by here.**
17 NSANGONG: **Wandered? They came on purpose, Shey.**
18   **Have you ever seen the owl beating its wings in**
19   **broad day?**
20 SHEY NGONG: **What then is their mission?**
21 NSANGONG: **Did you really speak? Shey, answer me.**
22   **Did you say anything offensive? Speak, Shey!**
23 SHEY NGONG: **Does it really matter, Nsangong? The**
24   **cat, no matter how full his stomach is, will never**
25   **spare the rat.**
26 NSANGONG: **But, did you say you are the iroko tree?**
27   **Shey, speak!**
28 SHEY NGONG: **He is not the sun that strides magistral**
29   **in the sky. We are not ants to be trampled**
30   **underfoot by the elephant.**
31 NSANGONG: **I fear and I tremble for you. Look, Shey,**
32   **get up. Let us go to the palace. Go and give the**
33   **monkey his banana. Or he will never give you**
34   **peace.**
35 SHEY NGONG: **The stream never flows uphill. The**

1   **leopard and the goat have never been bed-fellows.**
2   **I am waiting to hear from the palace.** *(A bugle*
3   *sounds so close that both of them are unnerved*
4   *momentarily. A messenger enters with "monkeng" and*
5   *walks towards SHEY NGONG.)*
6   MESSENGER: *(Handing over "monkeng")* **Greetings from**
7   **the Fon, Shey Ngong. And all his noble men. The**
8   **Fon desires your presence forthwith.**
9   SHEY NGONG: **Go back to your master and his family**
10   **of handclappers, and tell them that the stream**
11   **flows downhill.**
12   NSANGONG: **Wait a little, Shey. Consider what you say.**
13   SHEY NGONG: **You keep your mouth out of this,**
14   **Nsangong.** *(To MESSENGER)* **Tell your master that**
15   **the leopard and the goat have never eaten from the**
16   **same dish.**
17   MESSENGER: **But my lord, the lion of Ewawa means no**
18   **harm. Rather, he wants to share a cup with his**
19   **revered chief priest.**
20   NSANGONG: **That is the truth, Shey. The Fon means no**
21   **harm. But how could he? The cat and the dog may**
22   **quarrel over a piece of meat. But they are still**
23   **friends.**
24   SHEY NGONG: **I am no dog that will hunt for the**
25   **pleasure of another. The game must be shared. Let**
26   **every one have his fair share, I say. But your Fon**
27   **knows none other than his family and those that**
28   **come to him with gifts in return for the red feather.**
29   MESSENGER: **But, Shey, the Fon has refused you**
30   **nothing. All that remains is for you to ask.**
31   NSANGONG: **Is that not what I said? Shey, give the**
32   **monkey his banana. And take back your place**
33   **among the council of elders.**
34   MESSENGER: **That is all.**
35   SHEY NGONG: **Does the wise council ever discuss with**

1   the Fon? When the Fon pronounces that this farm-
2   land or that palm-bush now belongs to himself or
3   one of his family, does the wise council open its
4   mouth in disapproval? I spit on a body that only
5   gives approval and acclaims every decision taken
6   by one man.
7 NSANGONG: But Shey ...
8 MESSENGER: Watch your tongue, Shey. The Fon is the
9   wise one.
10 SHEY NGONG: Your Fon is the pig who knows only the
11   hunger of its own stomach.
12 MESSENGER: Eh? What did you say? Swallow your
13   words, Shey!
14 SHEY NGONG: I say your Fon is a goat ...
15 NSANGONG: Shey, please ...
16 MESSENGER: Is that so?
17 SHEY NGONG: And I am the stream that flows downhill.
18 MESSENGER: So be it. *(He sounds the bugle in mock honor*
19   *to SHEY NGONG, greets him in the traditional manner*
20   *reserved only for people of such status and exits with a*
21   *flourish.)*
22 NSANGONG: Shey, your sun has gone over the hill.
23 SHEY NGONG: And palm-wine will flow.
24 NSANGONG: You make light of serious matters, Shey.
25 SHEY NGONG: I do not make light of anything. But
26   since the Fon is the wise one ...
27 NSANGONG: *(Exits.)* I will follow him and keep my ears
28   close to the ground.
29 SHEY NGONG: *(Resuming his invocation)*
30   Oh! Nyombom!
31   Grant me strength,
32   Grant me wisdom,
33   Show me the right path
34   In this moment of trial ...
35   *(More distant shouts and ululations)* **Another red**

1   feather? Only Kibanya was due to be honored
2   today. When this land was still the land, empty
3   shells like Kibanya would never have had access to
4   the palace. Today, nobles have become slaves and
5   slaves nobles. Just because the late Fon ...
6   NSANGONG: *(Rushing in terribly agitated)* **Shey! Shey!**
7   Your wives' farmlands have been seized and given
8   to Kibanya's wives. A messenger is on the way to
9   deliver the Fon's pronouncement.
10   SHEY NGONG: Was that the reason for the recent
11   shouting and ululations?
12   NSANGONG: You heard them, Shey. You heard the
13   people rejoicing in your misfortune.
14   SHEY NGONG: That is what happens when there is
15   plenty of everything. The louse and the jigger have
16   no need for brains.
17   NSANGONG: My ear does not follow your tongue, Shey.
18   SHEY NGONG: When people overfeed like pigs and
19   soak themselves in palm-wine, they take pleasure
20   in desecrating their gods.
21   NSANGONG: You speak the truth, Shey. When there is
22   too much in the belly, the head becomes an empty
23   shell. *(Bugle sound followed by MESSENGER's*
24   *entrance)* **Your friend has arrived.**
25   MESSENGER: *(Mock greeting)* **Holy One, the lion of**
26   Ewawa has pronounced that the farmlands of your
27   revered wives now belong to Kibanya's wives.
28   SHEY NGONG: By whose order?
29   MESSENGER: Order? But I just told you. By the
30   pronouncement of the lion of Ewawa. The one you
31   have challenged to a wrestling match.
32   SHEY NGONG: The leopard does not wrestle with a goat.
33   MESSENGER: I am glad to hear that. The rat does not
34   play with the cat. I am glad you are beginning to
35   see reason.

1   SHEY NGONG: I am the leopard. I am the cat.

2   NSANGONG: How far can you carry this fight, Shey?

3   The forces against you are overwhelming.

4   MESSENGER: Yes, plead with your friend. Maybe he

5   will have an ear for what your tongue says.

6   SHEY NGONG: The gods and the ancestors will fight

7   their battle with the Fon. I am only their servant.

8   MESSENGER: Now that your wives have lost their

9   farmlands what are the gods and your ancestors

10   doing? *(One of the masks, Earth-Goddess, suddenly*

11   *becomes agitated and then pronounces.)*

12   EARTH-GODDESS: The sun shines on the hills.

13   The sun shines in the valleys.

14   The sun shines in the depths of the streams.

15   The sun shines.

16   MESSENGER: What was that?

17   NSANGONG: We are undone.

18   SHEY NGONG: The land has pronounced.

19   MESSENGER: What?

20   SHEY NGONG: The sun shines on the hills, in the

21   valleys and in the depths of the streams.

22   NSANGONG: A drought! A drought! We are undone.

23   SHEY NGONG: Hurry, fellow, and tell your master the

24   pronouncement of the land.

25   MESSENGER: You mean the gods have spoken?

26   NSANGONG: Do you or do you not have eyes and ears?

27   SHEY NGONG: You waste time. Haste to the wise one

28   and recount the happenings here.

29   NSANGONG: Go quickly.

30   MESSENGER: Very well. I will. *(Exits.)*

31   NSANGONG: I begin to believe in you, Shey. I will

32   follow him and keep my ears close to the ground.

33

34

35

Scene for
Two Females
and Two Males

Throwing Your Voice
by Craig Lucas

1   Murder is the subject of the opening scene in Craig Lucas's
2 *Throwing Your Voice* — which was first presented in 1991 in a
3 benefit for Amnesty International U.S.A.
4
5
6 **RICHARD: But to have them killed? Or maimed?**
7 **LUCY:** *(To Sarah)* **Some honey?** *(Sarah shakes her head.)*
8 **RICHARD: To pay somebody to do that for you? I mean, I**
9   **understand killing somebody in the heat of passion.**
10   **Or if they had something you really really wanted.**
11 **LUCY: They did.**
12 **DOUG: But they did.**
13 **RICHARD: I guess. I mean ... 'cause, but I actually have no**
14   **trouble imagining killing somebody when they walk in**
15   **the middle of the subway stairs in front of you really**
16   **slowly —**
17 **LUCY: Yes.**
18 **RICHARD: — and are just incredibly, *incredibly* fat —**
19 **SARAH: Watch it.**
20 **RICHARD: No, you know, you try to go this way, they**
21   **move —**
22 **DOUG: Right.**
23 **SARAH: They're doing it on purpose, just to incense you.**
24   *(Pause. The music plays.)*
25 **DOUG: ... Or those jerks who block the aisles at Food**
26   **Emporium, staring at some foodstuff —**
27 **RICHARD: Those are the ones.**
28 **DOUG: — as if they'd just woken up from a fifty-year sleep**
29   **and are trying to pick the really right ...**
30 **LUCY: They're having a stroke, probably.**

171

1   **DOUG:** *(Overlapping slightly)* **... brie ... . No, they're not**
2   **having a stroke. Why would you take their side? I**
3   **hate those people.**
4   **LUCY:** *(Smiles.)* **You're right. They should die.**
5   **RICHARD: I just ... I don't know ... to pay somebody ...**
6   **to kill the mother of your daughter's main**
7   **competition for the cheerleaders so she'll be too**
8   **distraught to audition ... It worries me.**
9   **DOUG: Well, it's passive aggressive.**
10 **LUCY: It is.**
11 **RICHARD:** *(To Sarah)* **Are we going to be like that in**
12   **sixteen years?**
13 **SARAH:** *(Nodding)* **Mm-hm.**
14 **RICHARD: Plotting ... living our entire lives through**
15   **little Grendel? Having no life of our own?**
16 **LUCY:** *(To Doug, overlapping from "Having — ")* **She**
17   **should've killed the daughter's friend directly.**
18 **DOUG: That would've been healthier.**
19
20
21
22
23
24
25
26
27
28
29
30
31
32
33
34
35

Scene for Four Females and Four Males

Fragments

by Edward Albee

1   Edward Albee is one of America's major dramatists. His 1962
2 New York Drama Critics Circle & Tony Award winning *Who's*
3 *Afraid of Virginia Woolf* is a classic of the contemporary theatre.
4 Three of his plays have won the Pulitzer Prize: *A Delicate Balance*
5 (1966); *Seascape* (1975); *Three Tall Women* (1991). *Fragments* is
6 the dramatist's commentary on the nature of fame.
7
8
9 MAN 4: **Edward Albee, who wrote this play, wanted you to**
10   **know about this charity auction — a sort of celebrity**
11   **auction he was asked to participate in.**
12 WOMAN 3: **Oh?**
13 MAN 4: **It was called Eggstravaganza, or some such thing.**
14 MAN 1: **How cute!**
15 MAN 4: *(To MAN 1)* **Now, now; never tell other people how**
16   **to run their lives — their charities, at any rate. It was**
17   **for a perfectly good charity, he says, and he gets**
18   **asked to do that sort of thing a lot, he says.**
19 MAN 2: **Unh-hunh; unh-hunh.**
20 WOMAN 2: **I've never done that.**
21 MAN 1: *(Looks at her oddly.)* **Of course not!**
22 WOMAN 1: **It must be fun!**
23 MAN 4: **He remembered that they sent him — and all the**
24   **others they asked, he imagined — a largish plastic egg**
25   **shell, sort of broken open, with some colored felt**
26   **pens, so he could decorate it as he wanted, and sign**
27   **his name, too.**
28 WOMAN 4: **That must have been a pretty big egg shell,**
29   **plastic or not — an ostrich egg?**
30 MAN 4: **I'm not sure. In any event ...**

1 MAN 1: Why didn't he just send a book of one of his
2   plays, or something? I'm sure he's got stacks of
3   them — remaindered, and all.
4 MAN 3: Now, now.
5 WOMAN 3: Yes: now, now.
6 MAN 4: I have no idea. Anyway, apparently what they
7   asked for was this ... egg shell, all decorated and
8   signed. And so, he did it ... appropriately, and so
9   did a lot of other celebrities.
10 WOMAN 2: What exactly is a celebrity these days?
11 WOMAN 3: Someone who gets asked to sign egg shells
12   and such. Shhhhh!
13 WOMAN 2: Oh!
14 MAN 4: Perhaps a hundred ... celebrities, and he did it,
15   and ... put it out of his mind.
16 MAN 1: ... As a proper celebrity would.
17 MAN 4: Yes.
18 WOMAN 4: *(To MAN 1)* There are limits to you.
19 MAN 1: *(To WOMAN 4)* Oh? There are? I haven't found
20   them.
21 MAN 4: May I finish this, please?
22 MAN 1: Oh, yeah.
23 WOMAN 4: Certainly. *("Have I stopped you?")*
24 MAN 4: And he said that one day he got this
25   mimeographed page of paper with — oh — lots of
26   names on it.
27 WOMAN 3: Mimeographed?
28 MAN 4: Well, Xeroxed is what he meant, probably.
29 MAN 3: Faxed, most likely.
30 MAN 4: Thank you. And there were all these names on
31   it — not alphabetized, though — with dollar
32   amounts next to them, and a little thank you note,
33   and he figured out that the dollar amounts were
34   what everybody's eggs had gotten at the charity
35   auction — what they had gone for. *(Smiles.)*

1   WOMAN 1: *(Urgent)* ... and!?
2   MAN 4: *(Thinking about something else.)* **Hm?**
3   WOMAN 1: And!?
4   MAN 4: Oh. Well, and naturally he looked to see where
5   he was — who got bid more for than him, who got
6   less — you know: natural curiosity.
7   WOMAN 1: AND!?
8   MAN 4: *(Smiles at her.)* And ... he made a note of the
9   interesting ones, and was surprised that he'd done
10   better than Glenn Close.
11 WOMAN 3: No!
12 MAN 4: *(Nods.)* Unh-hunh; and better than Victor Borge ...
13 MAN 3: Well, that's no surprise; isn't Victor Borge dead?
14 WOMAN 4: No, he is not!
15 WOMAN 1: Shhhhh!
16 MAN 4: ... And that he'd done better than Erma
17   Bombeck ...
18 WOMAN 2: Now, I can't believe that! Better than
19   Erma!?
20 MAN 2: Well, funny things happen.
21 WOMAN 2: Still!
22 MAN 4: ... And a lot better than Mortimer Adler.
23 MAN 1: Than who?
24 WOMAN 4: *(To MAN 4)* **Really!** *(To MAN 1)* **Where have**
25   **you been?** *(To MAN 4)* **Better than Mortimer Adler?**
26 WOMAN 1: *(To WOMAN 3)* Who is he?
27 WOMAN 3: He was a ... is a ... never mind.
28 MAN 4: Better than Jay Leno, better than Ralph Nader ...
29 MAN 2: Oh, come on!
30 MAN 4: Yep; better than Donald Trump, better than
31   Willard Scott ...
32 MAN 3: ... Even as we speak.
33 MAN 4: ... And better than Ted Danson ...
34 MAN 1: Where was this thing held — on Mars?
35 WOMAN 3: *(Giggles.)* Oh, hush!

177

1　MAN 4: ... And a lot of others, better than a lot of
2　　　　others, but those were the interesting ones.
3　MAN 2: Who did he do worse than?
4　WOMAN 1: Yes!
5　MAN 2: Whose egg did better?
6　MAN 4: Well, he thought that was very interesting. Aside
7　　　　from some people he'd never heard of — some
8　　　　locals, I guess — he was most impressed by three
9　　　　who'd done better — whose eggs had done better.
10　WOMAN 3: An important distinction.
11　WOMAN 4: *(To herself; grumpy)* **Better than Mortimer**
12　　　　**Adler. Really!**
13　MAN 3: Who did better? Whose egg did better?
14　MAN 4: Jean-Claude Van Damme, for one; Jean-Claude
15　　　　Van Damme did better.
16　MAN 3: Well, I suppose that figures.
17　MAN 2: Who else?
18　MAN 4: The Grateful Dead; they did a lot better.
19　MAN 2: Well ... naturally.
20　MAN 1: Of course.
21　WOMAN 1: And who else?
22　MAN 4: The one that got him the most, the one that
23　　　　impressed him most did better than he did —
24　　　　whose egg did better than he did ... than his did —
25　　　　was ... Don Knotts. *(Pause)*
26　MAN 3: *(Disbelief)* **No!**
27　WOMAN 3: You're joking.
28　MAN 2: Don Knotts!?
29　WOMAN 2: When was this thing held?
30　MAN 1: Mars.
31　WOMAN 2: Oh, right.
32　MAN 4: *(Pinning it down)* **Don ... Knotts.**
33　WOMAN 2: I declare.
34　MAN 4: He said that's the sort of thing puts it all in
35　　　　perspective for him — shrinks the head a little bit,

1   as he put it.

2   **WOMAN 4:** *(Shaking her head)* **I swear.**

3   **MAN 3: Don Knotts.**

4   **WOMAN 2: I ... I like Don Knotts.** *(They all look at her.)* **I**

5   **do!**

6   **MAN 1: Anybody do just the same as he did? — get bid**

7   **for the same?**

8   **MAN 4: Yes; there were three; three got the same bid he**

9   **did.**

10   **MAN 1: And ...?**

11   **MAN 4:** *(Without comment)* **Tim Conway, Ann Landers,**

12   **and Oliver North.** *(Silence)*

13   **MAN 3: I don't think there's anything more to say.**

14   **WOMAN 4: No. No.**

15   **WOMAN 3: No; certainly not. Poor Mr. Albee.**

16   **WOMAN 4: Yes; poor Mr. Albee.**

17   **MAN 1: Oh, these theatre people, the trouble they've**

18   **seen.**

19   **WOMAN 3: I tell you.**

20

21

22

23

24

25

26

27

28

29

30

31

32

33

34

35

Scene for
Any Gender

Tape

by José Rivera

1   What if you had to face the prospect of an eternity of listening
2 to your own lies? In *Tape*, which premiered at the Actors Theatre
3 in Louisville in 1993, José Rivera provides a glimpse of that
4 possibility. *Tape* is reprinted here in its entirety.

5

6

7   *A small dark room. No windows. One door. A PERSON is*
8   *being lead in by an ATTENDANT. In the room is a simple*
9   *wooden table and a chair. On the table is a large reel-to-reel*
10   *tape recorder, a glass of water, and a pitcher of water.*

11 **PERSON: It's dark in here.**

12 **ATTENDANT: I'm sorry.**

13 **PERSON: No, I know it's not your fault.**

14 **ATTENDANT: I'm afraid those lights ...**

15 **PERSON: I guess, what does it matter now?**

16 **ATTENDANT: ... Not very bright.**

17 **PERSON: Who cares, really?**

18 **ATTENDANT: We don't want to cause you any undue**
19   **suffering. If it's too dark in here for you I'll make sure**
20   **one of the other attendants replaces the light bulb.**

21 *(The PERSON looks at the ATTENDANT.)*

22 **PERSON: Any "undue suffering"?**

23 **ATTENDANT: That's right.** *(The PERSON looks at the room.)*

24 **PERSON: Is this where I'll be?**

25 **ATTENDANT: That's right.**

26 **PERSON: Will you be outside?**

27 **ATTENDANT: Yes.**

28 **PERSON: The entire time?**

29 **ATTENDANT: The entire time.**

30 **PERSON: Is it boring?**

1   ATTENDANT: *(As if the ATTENDANT hadn't heard)* **I'm**
2   **sorry?**
3   PERSON: **Is it boring? You know. Waiting outside all the**
4   **time.**
5   ATTENDANT: *(Soft smile)* **It's my job. It's what I do.**
6   PERSON: **Of course.** *(Beat)* **Will I get anything to eat or**
7   **drink?**
8   ATTENDANT: **Well, we're not really set up for that. We**
9   **don't have what you'd call a kitchen. But we can**
10   **send out for things. Little things. Cold food.**
11   PERSON: **I understand.**
12   ATTENDANT: **Soft drinks.**
13   PERSON: *(Hopefully)* **Beer?**
14   ATTENDANT: **I'm afraid not**
15   PERSON: **Not even on special occasions like my birthdays?**
16   ATTENDANT: *(Thinking)* **I guess maybe on your birthday.**
17   PERSON: *(Truly appreciative)* **Great. Thanks.** *(Beat)*
18   ATTENDANT: **Do you have any more questions before**
19   **we start? Because if you do, that's OK. It's OK to**
20   **ask as many questions as you want. I'm sure you're**
21   **very curious. I'm sure you'd like to know as much**
22   **as possible, so you can figure out how it all fits**
23   **together and what it all means. So please ask.**
24   **That's why I'm here. Don't worry about the time.**
25   **We have a lot of time.** *(Beat)*
26   PERSON: **I don't have any questions.**
27   ATTENDANT: *(Disappointed)* **Are you sure?**
28   PERSON: **There's not much I really have to know is**
29   **there? Really?**
30   ATTENDANT: **No, I guess not. I just thought ...**
31   PERSON: **It's OK. I appreciate it. I guess I really want**
32   **to sit.**
33   ATTENDANT: **Sit.** *(The PERSON sits on the chair and faces*
34   *the tape recorder.)*
35   PERSON: **OK, I'm sitting.**

1 ATTENDANT: Is it ... comfortable?
2 PERSON: Does it matter? Does it really fucking matter?
3 ATTENDANT: No. I suppose not. *(The ATTENDANT looks*
4   *sad. The PERSON looks at the ATTENDANT and feels*
5   *bad.)*
6 PERSON: Hey I'm sorry. I know it's not your fault I
7   know you didn't mean it. I'm sorry.
8 ATTENDANT: It's all right.
9 PERSON: What's your name anyway? Do you have a
10   name?
11 ATTENDANT: Not really. It's not allowed.
12 PERSON: Really? Not allowed? Who says?
13 ATTENDANT: The rules say.
14 PERSON: Have you actually seen these rules? Are they
15   in writing?
16 ATTENDANT: Oh yes. There's a long and extensive
17   training course.
18 PERSON: *(Surprised)* There is?
19 ATTENDANT: Oh yes. It's quite rigorous.
20 PERSON: Imagine that.
21 ATTENDANT: You have to be a little bit of everything.
22   Confidant, confessor, friend, stern task master,
23   guide.
24 PERSON: I guess that would take time.
25 ATTENDANT: My teachers were all quite strong and
26   capable. They really pushed me. I was grateful. I
27   knew I had been chosen for something unique and
28   exciting. Something significant. Didn't mind the
29   hard work and sleepless nights.
30 PERSON: *(Surprised)* Oh? You sleep?
31 ATTENDANT: *(Smiles.)* When I can. *(Beat)*
32 PERSON: Do you dream? *(Beat)*
33 ATTENDANT: No. *(Beat)* That's not allowed. *(Beat)*
34 PERSON. I'm sorry.
35 ATTENDANT: No. It's something you get used to.

1   PERSON: *(Trying to be chummy)* **I know I went years and**
2   **years without being able to remember one single**
3   **dream I had. It really scared the shit out of me**
4   **when I was ten and ...**
5   ATTENDANT: **I know.**
6   PERSON: **I'm sorry.**
7   ATTENDANT: **I said I know. I know that story. When you**
8   **were ten.**
9   PERSON: **Oh. Yeah. I guess you would know everything.**
10   **Every story.**
11   ATTENDANT: *(Apologetic)* **It's part of the training.**
12   PERSON: **I figured.** *(A long uncomfortable silence)*
13   ATTENDANT: *(Softly)* **Have you ever operated a reel-to-**
14   **reel tape recorder before?**
15   PERSON: *(Suddenly terrified)* **No I haven't. I mean — no.**
16   ATTENDANT: **It's not hard.**
17   PERSON: **I, uhm, these things were pretty obsolete by**
18   **the time I was old enough to afford stereo**
19   **equipment, you know, I got into cassettes and,**
20   **later, CDs, but never one of these jobbies.**
21   ATTENDANT: **It's not hard.** *(Demonstrates.)* **On here. Off**
22   **here. Play. Pause. Rewind.**
23   PERSON: *(Surprised)* **Rewind?**
24   ATTENDANT: **In some cases the quality of the recording**
25   **is so poor ... you'll want to rewind it until you**
26   **understand.**
27   PERSON: **No fast forward?**
28   ATTENDANT: **No.**
29   PERSON: *(Getting progressively more frightened)* **It looks**
30   **like a pretty good one. Sturdy. Very strong.**
31   ATTENDANT: **They get a lot of use.**
32   PERSON: **I bet.** *(Beat)* **Is this the only tape?** *(The*
33   *ATTENDANT laughs out loud — then quickly stops.)*
34   ATTENDANT: **No.**
35   PERSON: **I didn't think so.**

1   ATTENDANT: There are many more.

2   PERSON: How many? A lot?

3   ATTENDANT: There are ten thousand boxes.

4   PERSON: Ten thousand?

5   ATTENDANT: I'm afraid so.

6   PERSON: Did I really ... did I really lie that much?

7   ATTENDANT: I'm afraid you did.

8   PERSON: So ... everyone goes into a room like this?

9   ATTENDANT: Exactly   like   this.   There's   no

10   differentiation. Everyone's equal.

11   PERSON: For once.

12   ATTENDANT: What isn't equal, of course, is the ...

13   amount of time you spend here. Listening.

14   PERSON: *(Horror stricken)* **Oh God.**

15   ATTENDANT: *(Part of the training)* **Listening, just to**

16   **yourself. To your voice.**

17   PERSON: I know.

18   ATTENDANT: Listening, word by word, to every lie you

19   ever told while you were alive.

20   PERSON: Oh God!

21   ATTENDANT: Every ugly lie to every person, every

22   single time, every betrayal, every lying thought,

23   every time you lied to yourself, deep in your mind,

24   we were listening, we were recording, and it's all in

25   these tapes, ten thousand boxes of them, in your

26   own words, one lie after the next, over and over,

27   until we're finished. So the amount of time varies.

28   The amount of time you spend here all depends on

29   how many lies you told. How many boxes of tapes

30   we have to get through together.

31   PERSON: *(Almost in tears)* I'm sorry...

32   ATTENDANT: Too late.

33   PERSON: I said I'm sorry! I said I'm sorry! I said it a

34   million times! What happened to forgiveness?! I

35   don't want to be here! I don't want this! I don't

1   **want to listen! I don't want to hear myself. I didn't**
2   **mean to say the things that I said! I don't want to**
3   **listen!**
4   **ATTENDANT: Yes, well. Neither did we. Neither did we.**
5   *(The ATTENDANT looks sadly at the PERSON. The*
6   *ATTENDANT turns on the tape recorder. The*
7   *ATTENDANT hits the "Play" button, the reels spin*
8   *slowly, and the tape starts snaking its way through the*
9   *machine. Silence. The ATTENDANT leaves the room,*
10   *leaving the PERSON all alone. The PERSON nervously*
11   *pours a glass of water, accidentally spilling water on the*
12   *floor. From the depths of the machine comes a long-*
13   *forgotten voice.)*
14 **WOMAN'S VOICE: Where have you been? Do you know**
15   **I've been looking all over? Jesus Christ! I went to**
16   **Manny's! I went to the pharmacy! The school! I**
17   **even called the police! Look at me, Jesus Christ,**
18   **I'm shaking! Now look at me — look at me and tell**
19   **me where the hell you were! Tell me right now!**
20   *(Silence. As the PERSON waits, terrified and sad, for*
21   *the lying response, the lights fade to black.)*
22
23
24
25
26
27
28
29
30
31
32
33
34
35

Permissions Acknowledgments

public reading, radio broadcasting, television, video or sound taping, all other forms of mechanical or electronic reproduction, such as information storage and retrieval systems and photocopying, and the rights of translation into foreign languages, are strictly reserved. Particular emphasis is laid upon the question of readings, permission for which must be secured from the Author's agent in writing. Inquiries concerning all rights should be addressed to the Author's agent, The Tantleff Office, Inc., 375 Greenwich Street, Suite 700, New York, NY 10013."

NIGHTMARE by Steven H. Gale. Copyright © 1999 by Steven H. Gale.

UNANSWERED INVOCATION by Shannon Gale. Copyright © 1999 by Shannon Gale.

IN SHAKESPEARE AND THE BIBLE by Thornton Wilder. Copyright © 1997 by A. Tappan Wilder, Catharine K. Wilder and Catherine W. Guiles. Reprinted by permission of the Wilder Family LLC and the Barbara Hogenson Agency.

PRIVATE EYES by Steven Dietz. Copyright © 1998, by Steven Dietz. CAUTION: Professionals and amateurs are hereby warned that **PRIVATE EYES** is subject to royalty. It is fully protected under the copyright laws of the United States of America, the British Commonwealth, including Canada, and all other countries of the Copyright Union. All rights, including professional, amateur, motion picture, recitation, lecturing, public reading, radio broadcasting, television, and the rights of translation into foreign languages are strictly reserved. In its present form the play is dedicated to the reading public only.

The amateur and stock live stage performance rights to **PRIVATE EYES** are controlled exclusively by Dramatists Play Service, Inc. at 440 Park Avenue South, New York, New York 10016.

For all other rights than those stipulated above, apply to Sarah Jane Leigh, International Creative Management, 40 West 57th Street, 18th Floor, New York, New York 10019.

CLOUD TECTONICS by José Rivera. Copyright © 1997 by José Rivera.

MISREADINGS by Neena Beber. Copyright © by Neena Beber.

SLAVS! by Tony Kushner. Excerpt from *Thinking About The Longstanding Problems Of Virtue* and *Happiness* by Tony Kushner. Copyright © 1995. Reprinted by Permission of Theatre Communications Group.

BELOW THE BELT by Richard Dresser. Copyright © 1995, 1997 by Richard Dresser. ALL RIGHTS RESERVED. CAUTION: Professionals and amateurs are hereby warned that **BELOW THE BELT** is subject to a royalty. It is fully protected under the copyright laws of the United States of America, the British commonwealth, including Canada, and all other countries of the Copyright Union. All rights, including professional, amateur, motion pictures, recitation, lecturing, public reading, radio broadcasting, television, and the rights of translation into foreign languages are strictly reserved. In its present form the play is dedicated to the reading public only.

The amateur live stage performance rights to **BELOW THE BELT** are controlled exclusively by Samuel French, Inc. and royalty arrangements and licenses must be secured well in advance of presentation. PLEASE NOTE that amateur royalty fees are set upon application in accordance with your producing circumstances. When applying for a royalty quotation and license please give us the number of performances intended, dates of production, your seating capacity and admission fee. Royalties are payable one week before the opening performance of the play to Samuel French, Inc., at 45 W. 25th Street, New York, NY 10010; or at 7623 Sunset Blvd., Hollywood, CA 90046, or to Samuel French (Canada), Ltd., 100 Lombard Street, Toronto, Ontario, Canada M5C JM3.

PORNO by Mario Fratti. Copyright © 1990 by Mario Fratti. Mario Fratti is a drama critic and a playwright. He was born in Italy but has been living in New York City since 1963. His plays *Cage, Suicide, Return, Refusal, Refrigerators, Academy, Seducers, Victim, Che Guevara, Young Wife, Birthday, Mothers and Daughters, Eleonora Duse, Mafia, Gift, Races, Bridge, Lovers, Friends, Encounter, A.I.D.S., Porno, Two Centuries, Dolls No More, Family, Sister, Leningrad, Passionate Women,* have been performed in more than six hundred theatres in nineteen languages. The musical *Nine* (his adaptation of Fellini's film *8 1/2*) won the ONeill Selection Award, the Richard Rodgers Award, The Outer Critics Circle Award, the Leone di San Marco Literary Award, the Heritage and Culture Award, eight Drama Desk Awards and five Tony Awards.

About the Editor

Steven H. Gale received his B.A. from Duke University (where he participated in Duke Players productions), his M.A. from the University of California at Los Angeles, and his Ph.D. from the University of Southern California. He has taken post-graduate courses at several universities, including MIT and Oxford University (Christ Church). He has taught at UCLA, USC, the University of Puerto Rico, the University of Liberia (as a Fulbright Professor of American and British Literature and Director of University Players), the University of Florida, Missouri Southern State, and Kentucky State University (he is the University Endowed Chair in the Humanities). Besides 20 scholarly books and 150 articles on drama, film, folktales, and British, American, and African literature, he has published short stories, poetry, and one-act plays. Gale is internationally recognized as the leading authority on the works of Harold Pinter (eleven books, including the standard bibliography and *Butter's Going Up: A Critical Analysis of Harold Pinter's Work*, one of the first major monographs on Pinter); he was the founding president of the Harold Pinter Society and is a founding co-editor of *The Pinter Review: Annual Essays*. Gale has also acted in local productions and directed both university players and small theatre groups, and he has taught a course in acting. He is currently working on a study of Pinter's screenplays, a novel, and a screenplay.

Order Form

Meriwether Publishing Ltd.
P.O. Box 7710
Colorado Springs, CO 80933
Telephone: (719) 594-4422
Website: www.meriwetherpublishing.com

Please send me the following books:

_____ **Outstanding Stage Monologs and** $14.95
Scenes from the '90s   #BK-B236
edited by Steven H. Gale
Professional auditions for student actors

_____ **Audition Scenes for Student Actors #BK-B232** $15.95
edited by Roger Ellis
Selections from contemporary plays

_____ **Scenes and Monologs from the Best** $14.95
New Plays   #BK-B140
edited by Roger Ellis
An anthology of new American plays

_____ **The Scenebook for Actors   #BK-B177** $15.95
edited by Norman A. Bert
Collection of great monologs and dialogs for auditions

_____ **Great Scenes from** $15.95
Minority Playwrights   #BK-B207
edited by Marsh Cassady
Seventy-four scenes of cultural diversity

_____ **Playing Contemporary Scenes   #BK-B100** $16.95
edited by Gerald Lee Ratliff
Thirty-one famous scenes and how to play them

_____ **The Theatre Audition Book   #BK-B224** $16.95
by Gerald Lee Ratliff
*Playing monologs from contemporary, modern,
period and classical plays*

These and other fine Meriwether Publishing books are available at
your local bookstore or direct from the publisher. Prices subject to
change without notice. Check our website or call for current prices.

Name: _____

Organization name: _____

Address: _____

City: _____ State: _____

Zip: _____ Phone: _____
  ❑ **Check Enclosed**
  ❑ **Visa / MasterCard / Discover #** _____
                              Expiration
Signature: _____ date: _____
      (required for Visa/MasterCard orders)

Colorado residents: Please add 3% sales tax.
Shipping: Include $2.75 for the first book and 50¢ for each additional book ordered.

  ❑ *Please send me a copy of your complete catalog of books and plays.*